# Trapped Between Two Worlds

*Sandra Ramdhanie*

# Trapped Between Two Worlds

Experiences of a 'Ghost Buster'

SANDRA RAMDHANIE

THE O'BRIEN PRESS
DUBLIN

This edition first published 1995 by The O'Brien Press Ltd.,
20 Victoria Road, Rathgar, Dublin 6, Ireland.

Copyright © Sandra Ramdhanie

All rights reserved. No part of this book may be reproduced
or utilised in any way or by any means, electronic or mechanical,
including photocopying, recording or by any information storage
and retrieval system without permission in writing from the
publisher. This book may not be sold as a bargain book
or at a reduced rate without permission in
writing from the publisher.

2 4 6 8 10 9 7 5 3 1
96 98 00 02 04 03 01 99 97 95

British Library Cataloguing-in-Publication Data
Ramdhanie, Sandra
Trapped Between Two Worlds
I. Title
133.9

ISBN 0-86278-384-4

Editing, design and typesetting: The O'Brien Press
Cover illustration: Tom Byrne
Cover design: Neasa Ní Chianáin
Separations: Lithoset
Printing: Cox & Wyman, Reading

# Contents

Introduction 7

My Little Green Man 9

*Obeah* Man and *La Diablesse* 21

Spirit Cats and Black Dogs 32

Stephen Moves on to the Light 49

The World of the Spirit 61

Solving the 'Halloween Case' 77

How to Tune in to your Inner Energies 90

Techniques in Spirit Work 100

The Powers of Crystals and Stones 113

Seeing into the Past 129

'Tuning in' to County Wicklow 137

The House of Many Spirits 146

# Introduction

GHOST STORIES HAVE BEEN TOLD and retold since the beginning of time, an inherent part of every culture. My wish in recording some of my own experiences of spiritual phenomena is to shed a little light on the area of ghosts and hauntings, poltergeists and apparitions. As a parapsychologist I investigate cases of this nature; as a psychic I communicate with spirits who are 'trapped between two worlds', and as a healer I help them to move on to the Afterworld.

I can truthfully say I have never encountered an 'evil' spirit, perhaps because I believe that evil, like beauty, is in the eye of the beholder. Nor have I ever heard of anyone being hurt or injured in any way by a spirit. The most common way of dealing with spirit presence in Ireland is by exorcism, which I see as a form of attack not appropriate in many cases. You could say the exorcist attempts to 'evict' the spirits while I do my best to 're-house' them. They were once human beings like ourselves, and as such deserve to be treated with more than the fear and ignorance they seem to inspire.

The cases reported in this book are all true, though some names and locations have been changed at the request of the individuals concerned. The exercises and techniques described here can be used for relaxation, healing and psychic development. They are best recorded on to an audio cassette, you can then tune in to your own voice as it leads you into a state of relaxation.

These exercises are NOT a blueprint for clearing a house of spirits, and I do not recommend enthusiasts to try my methods unless they already have experience in this field. While I have not encountered any frightening situations, I cannot guarantee that others will be equally lucky.

*Sandra Ramdhanie*

## CHAPTER 1

# My Little Green Man

IT WAS A NIGHTLY RITUAL. My mother would put me to bed, turn out the light – despite my pleas – and shut the door. The bedroom was large and dark and I was only three years old. I would snuggle under the bedclothes immediately and lie there terrified, clutching my pillow for comfort and hoping I would not die of suffocation as my mother had warned.

Then, all of a sudden, I would feel a peaceful calm steal over me and I knew I could relax because my friend was there. My friend was green and about two feet tall. He always appeared in the same spot, on top of a tallboy near the window. His skin, hair and clothes were all a uniform shade of bright, grassy green.

We communicated in a way which I would later come to identify as intuitive rather than telepathic – that is, we sent each other feelings rather than thoughts. No words were involved as none was needed. He made me feel safe and secure. We liked each other. These were the basic messages conveyed between us. I would sleep soundly then, knowing my friend was there watching over me. He stopped appearing when my brother was put to sleep in the bedroom with me.

Despite the disbelief of my parents and other adults, I knew my little green man was real. Years later, in Celtic countries and in Germany, I discovered references to a form of nature spirit, known as the Green Man, identical in description to my little friend. This was the first of many incidents and occurrences that I now know were psychic although I could not recognise them as such at the time.

Children are incredibly intuitive beings: we are much more in touch with our psychic senses before the age of seven. Children also accept things without questioning them. It did not seem at all unusual to me that my friend was green, just as the children I now encounter while investigating paranormal activities in houses accept their 'spirit friends'.

I was born feet first, despite the efforts of my mother's doctor who had turned me around several times in the womb. Less than one percent of children are born like this and folklore has it that they are psychic. The date of my birth – 1 November – is also significant. This is the Feast of All Hallows or *Samhain*, the time of the year traditionally associated with psychic and spirit matters. As with any other talent, psychic abilities tend to run in families. In retrospect, I now realise that both my parents – an Irish mother and an Indian father – were very intuitive people, although they openly profess to be sceptics. When I was six weeks old, they brought me from England, where I was born, to Ireland. We lived in Elgin Road, Ballsbridge, in Dublin, and this is where my little green man visited me.

My mother tells me that when I learned to speak, at a little over a year old, I objected to being called Sandra and insisted that I was a male Chinese doctor called Dr Wu. I was obviously remembering a previous existence, although I have no recall of that life now. As infants we remember our past lives and mothers often notice this at a subconscious level. How often have we heard the phrase 'He's been here before' being used by a proud mum? We in Ireland are in tune on a subtle level with the concept of reincarnation, although many will say that they don't believe in it.

My father was a medical student at the College of Surgeons in Dublin and many of his student friends used to come to our house to study. On one occasion, when I was three years old, they were asking each other questions from previous years' exam papers. Apparently, I astounded them by knowing the answers, complex medical terms coming from the mouth of a three year old. This further convinced my parents that I had been a doctor in a past life. There is a theory among those who, like myself, work in the field of reincarnation that, when a soul decides to reincarnate, it chooses its parents for the particular qualities it needs in its new life. It may be that I chose my father because of his involvement in medicine.

Certainly, my one ambition during childhood was to be a doctor when I grew up, to help people and to make them better. I was healing intuitively from a very early age, although I could not have put a name to what I was doing. It was like a burning belief from within that I could make someone better by willing it and by touch. When I was about six years old, my brother, Richard, found an injured jackdaw and brought it home. I used to hold it in my hands and will it to get better. I really believed this would heal it. I did the same thing many times as a child as members of our family of animal lovers were constantly bringing home injured creatures.

My dreams, too, were always colourful and significant, often predicting trivial events or experiences. We had an Alsatian dog called Gerry and one night I dreamt I saw him with his tongue split in half. Several weeks later, he cut his tongue on the latch of the gate in the back garden. The tongue healed with a split in the middle, exactly as I had seen it in my dream.

I had another dream of a large golden-brown teddy-bear with a red bow round his neck. Months later, I saw him in a shop near my grandmother's house in Booterstown Avenue. He was the first prize in a raffle and to my amazement my grandmother won him and gave him to me. Afterwards I heard my parents discussing how she had bought every ticket in the raffle, knowing how much I wanted him!

Some of my earliest memories involve seeing my great-grandmother gardening and tending her house plants. As a young woman she had a strange experience, which was recounted to me by my grandmother, Emily. My great-grandmother simply 'disappeared into thin air' one day. She had been sitting out in the back garden, but when her mother went out to look for her, she was nowhere to be found. No-one had seen her pass through the house to go out the front door and nobody had the faintest idea where she might be.

She remained missing for a week, during which time no news of any kind about her was heard. Eventually she was found in the back garden in a semi-conscious condition in the place where she had last been seen. She was put to bed, where she remained for several weeks, unable to speak, seeming weak but otherwise physically healthy. Every doctor and priest in the neighbourhood visited her in an attempt to solve the mystery of her disappearance.

Finally, a young priest new to the parish called to the house.

On seeing him, she sat up and announced in a loud voice: 'I know who you are.' She then proceeded to tell him the names of his family members, where he lived and many other things about himself that only he could know. She recovered after that and in time the incident was forgotten. My grandmother was convinced that she had been taken away by aliens on a UFO and had developed psychic abilities as a result. The episode has remained a mystery to this day.

A couple of weeks before my great-grandmother died, my great-grandfather fell ill and was confined to bed. My grandmother tells me that she arrived home one night during this time, opened the front door, and immediately the dog started barking and growling furiously. He was looking at a spot behind her in the open doorway. Both my great-grandmother and my grandmother stared as the dog seemed to watch something come into the hall and go upstairs. 'That's death come for your father,' said my great-grandmother.

But her final prediction proved wrong. She herself was the one who died two weeks later. Loud scratching, like rats behind the walls – another common Irish death warning – had also been heard in the house for weeks before.

I remember the night she died. I was seven years old. The family were all asleep in bed when we were woken by the sound of loud knocking on the front door. My mother opened her bedroom window and looked down but there was no-one to be seen on the doorstep or in the garden. Again we heard the knock; again my mother looked out to see an empty doorstep. She did not seem surprised next morning to hear that her grandmother had died during the night at the exact time we heard the knocking on the door.

My grandmother, Emily, was a voracious reader and had a

particular interest in the native American Indians. She knew about the different Indian nations and their customs and delighted in spotting inaccuracies in the Wild West films she loved to watch. I often stayed with her during the periods when my father was studying for exams and these were some of the happiest days of my childhood.

Emily was fascinated by ghost stories and I would listen with excitement and delicious fear to the tales being told around me. One of them concerned my mother who was an only child and when very young went to spend the night in her aunt's house in Blackrock. She woke in the middle of the night screaming and crying and told her aunt she had seen a coalman looking in the window. My grand-aunt later confided to my grandmother that she herself had seen someone who looked like a coalman walking through one wall of the house and out through the opposite one. She ran to the window and looked out but could see no sign of him. She was very shaken by this incident and mentioned it to her neighbours. Several of them said they too had sometimes seen a 'dirty-looking man' who seemed to disappear into the wall of the house. My grand-aunt said the 'coalman' did not pay any attention to her; in fact, she thought he could not even see her.

There was a large convent with rambling grounds not far from where my grandmother lived and many of the local girls worked there for the nuns. Emily knew an old lady who had been one of the maids and who swore she had to leave because the house attached to the convent was haunted. One day, she said, she was in the sitting-room with the Mother Superior, who asked her to open the front door as someone was coming. She looked out of the window to see a tall man, dressed in black and wearing a top hat, who appeared to be walking about a foot above the level of the drive. When she opened the front door, however, there was nobody in sight and an explanation was never found.

A few weeks later, the same woman awoke in the middle of the night to see a priest saying Mass on a little table at the end of the room. She woke the maid who shared the room with her and she too, saw the same sight. Both girls ran out of the room screaming, rousing several members of the household in their fright. When they went back to the room, accompanied by two nuns, there was nothing unusual to be seen. The maids immediately gave in their notice. Later, they found out that the house had once been occupied by a family who had hidden a priest in their 'priests' hole' during the Penal Law days of eighteenth-century Ireland when the saying of Mass was forbidden and priests were hunted down and executed. The priest had lived in a little room with a hidden entrance through the room that the girls had been sleeping in. He used to come out of his hiding-place occasionally to say Mass for his host family on the same table the girls had seen him using. Many old houses in Ireland have similar secret rooms where a priest or other fugitive could be concealed when necessary.

That particular house had been on the market a long time before the nuns bought it, as there had always been rumours of 'strange goings-on' connected with it. One prospective buyer had taken his wife to the estate agent to enquire about viewing the property. The agent gave them a key to have a look, saying he would join them in a few minutes. The couple went to the house and took their time looking around downstairs. As there was still no sign of the agent, they went upstairs and into the first bedroom on the landing. They heard heavy footsteps cross the hall and walk up the stairs and went out onto the landing to greet the estate agent, as they thought. There was nobody in sight. As they stood frozen to the spot, staring at each other, they heard a key turn in the front door and the estate agent walked in. He was amazed to see the terrified couple running down the stairs towards him and even more amazed when the husband thrust the key into his hand as he ran out the door, shouting: 'That house is troubled.'

My grandmother also knew an old gardener who lived with his wife and tubercular son in a small cottage on the land owned by the nuns. The son helped his father with less strenuous tasks. One day he climbed up into the large apple-loft on his way back from picking apples in the orchard. Hearing his father climb up the ladder after him, he called to him to bring up the hammer. He turned around on hearing the footsteps reach the top of the ladder and got the shock of his life when he saw no-one there. In his fright, he jumped out of the loft to the ground instead of using the ladder, and broke his leg.

My grandmother came from Maynooth, Co. Kildare, and had some interesting stories about that area. One of them concerned a man well-known in the county for playing the tin whistle. One evening, he was lying sunning himself in a field, a few yards from a fairy fort. He fell asleep and woke up inside the fairy hill, surrounded by tiny people, about two feet tall, who were playing musical instruments and dancing. They asked him to play the whistle for them and brought him food and drink.

He was just going to take a bite when he heard a voice in his ear say: 'Eat nor drink nothing here.' He refused the food and drink and commenced to play the whistle. The little people danced and feasted for what seemed like several hours until finally he told them he wanted to go home. They urged him to stay but, when he insisted on leaving, they presented him with a solid gold whistle. When he got home, he discovered that a full twenty-four hours had passed since he fell asleep. After this adventure, he became even more famous for his whistle playing and many heard and remarked on the glorious, unearthly tones of his fairy whistle.

My grandmother had two old letters from her brother who was soldiering in India, which indicate the existence of psychic abilities in my ancestors. The first concerned a strange experience he had while on sentry duty one night. He was standing alone in the dark when suddenly his mother appeared before him. She looked solemnly at him for several seconds, then smiled sweetly and disappeared. The second letter, dated some months later, thanked my grandmother for her letter in which she told him of their mother's death. He remarked how strange it was that he had seen his mother appear at what seemed to be the exact moment of her passing. (This is a point-of-death apparition as described in Chapter 5.)

You could say I cut my teeth on tales such as these and I must admit I drank in every word of these mysterious stories eagerly. But I was always puzzled by the fact that in many haunted houses some of the residents never noticed or encountered anything unusual. I now believe that this is because only some of us possess the heightened sensitivity necessary to experience psychic phenomena strongly. However, I am convinced that every human being is born with some form of psychic ability which, in most cases, may simply be intuition, that gut feeling that alerts you to the fact that something is going to happen. In Chapter 7, I describe the various forms this ability can take and how it can be developed effectively by each one of us.

Children, as I have mentioned earlier, have no trouble with understanding psychic matters and concepts such as healing by laying on of hands are perfectly normal to their eyes. They do not question as adults do, which makes them more open as well as more vulnerable. I was giving some healing to a friend in my kitchen recently when my six-year-old son, Taran, came into the room and automatically joined in. I have never encouraged my children to get involved in any of my work but I said nothing and observed him. He used regular, sweeping movements of his hands in a manner totally unlike my own but which I have seen other healers use. What amazed me was the confident way he went about it, as if he knew exactly what he was doing.

From the time she was a baby, my daughter, Tanith, also had a natural grasp of the healing concept. She would ask me to put my hands on her if she was ill or hurt; sometimes she would just take my hand and put it on the sore spot. Children know, on an inner level, that the touch of their mother's hands makes them feel better. Most mothers have healing ability, which is simply an input of positive energy from one person to another.

I believe that people who are in close contact with nature and the soil have strong healing energy and intuition as a result. Many gardeners and farmers, for example, have a very developed energy which they transmit through their hands to the plants or animals they are tending. In the US, many years of research in this area have established its effectiveness. Laboratory experiments such as the following (which you can try at home) prove that every human being possesses this ability, not just the chosen few. Two identical rows of seedlings are watered from the same jug of water. Row A is watered first, then the container with the remaining water is held in the hands for five to ten minutes before watering Row B. The seedlings from Row B will generally grow approximately twice as fast as those in Row A. You can also try watering half your house plants with energised water and watch for the difference. As you hold the container, picture, in your mind's eye, bright, golden light pouring from your hands into the water. This is known as 'charged' or energised water. Drinking charged water is good for a variety of health problems, expecially those of the digestive system.

This type of experiment was not carried out using healers or anyone in the healing arts and it demonstrates that, as human beings, we all possess healing energy which we can transmit through our hands. If, by simply touching something, we transmit an energy to it, then how much more effective can it be if we develop and direct this energy? The actual effect can now be photographed using Kirlian photography in which the energy shows up as a white light glowing around the fingers.

I was an avid reader as a child. When I was nine, my father bought me a book that was to change my life. It was *The Last Days of Pompeii* by Lord Lytton. I plunged into the world of the ancient Roman Empire and lived every moment of the book. I read it nine times, one after the other, and seemed incapable of tiring of this ancient world. The villain of the piece is a priest called Arbaces of the ancient Egyptian religion of Isis. I felt instinctively that a priest of Isis shouldn't be evil and I gradually came to the realisation, as I read more and more about Egypt, that I had lived there in ancient times as a priestess of Isis. At that early age, I developed a passion for Egypt and for Greek and Roman mythology that remains with me to this day.

Studying Latin and Roman history in secondary school reinforced this interest. I was attending Loreto College and the fact that my mother was an atheist and my father a Presbyterian was a distinct disadvantage in that environment. It was here, however, at the age of fourteen, that I was first made aware of my ability as a clairvoyant. The school was holding a big fund-raising bazaar and the nuns appointed me to be the fortune-teller. I didn't think the people 'consulting' me would be expecting the real thing and I certainly wasn't taking it seriously. I dressed for the role in gaudy scarves and enormous earrings, daringly blew cigarette smoke into the upturned goldfish bowl which was to be my crystal ball and played my part for the day.

A few weeks later the feedback started. People began to tell me that the things I had predicted had come true. Parents who had heard what happened wanted to consult me. The sheer amount of the feedback from pupils and parents started me wondering whether it was, in fact, possible to predict the future. I got a book on palmistry from the library and learned from it how to read the lines on the hand. I studied the lines on my own hand and used this as a guideline for reading the palms of other people. My own lines pointed to my talents being medical, psychic and literary – all areas which have fascinated me all my life.

## CHAPTER 2

# Obeah Man and La Diablesse

WHEN I WAS SEVENTEEN, MY FAMILY went to live in Trinidad, a Caribbean island seven miles from Venezuela. The lush, tropical beauty of the place was a dazzling contrast to the soft green of our Irish countryside. The people seemed gay and carefree, due, I now believe, to absorbing all that lovely sun energy. My lifestyle changed considerably. I began studying pharmacy at the University of the West Indies in St Augustine and working as a student-pharmacist in the dispensary of San Fernando General Hospital.

San Fernando is the industrial capital of the island and this is where we lived when we first arrived. It was here I became aware of the local tradition of *obeah*, which is similar to Haitian *voodoo* though less sinister than the image the media likes to portray. *Obeah* consists of the usual spells, curses and potions which are the stock-in-trade of the *shaman* or medicine man the world over.

My father owned a drugstore, or chemist shop as we call them. Every day customers came in to fill their 'prescriptions' from the local *obeah* man. Requests for love powder, commanding powder and dragon's blood were frequent, along with many other exotic-sounding compounds. Almost all the pharmacies in Trinidad stock these to meet the enormous demand among the Afro-Caribbean community.

Many of the inhabitants of the Caribbean islands have African blood. Their ancestors were taken as slaves from Africa, bringing with them a belief in their old gods, goddesses and religious rituals. These have been inherited by succeeding generations and combined with elements of Catholicism to form a belief system widespread in the Caribbean and South American countries to the present day. In Cuba this belief is known as *la santeria*; in Haiti as *voodoo* or *vodun*; in Jamaica, Trinidad and Tobago as *obeah* or *obi*; and in some of the other islands it is called *shango* or *chango*. There exists, of course, a wide range of regional variations, but certain practices are common to all. The religious ceremonies involve dancing to the rhythm of the drum until a trance-like state is reached, leading to the possession of dancers by gods known as *loa*, *mysteres* or *saints*. The first *loa* to 'possess' a devotee becomes chief of his or her personal gods. Believers feel that their own spirit is displaced by that of the *loa* during possession, and they undergo radical personality changes in accordance with the nature of the deity. Blood sacrifice, usually in the form of a black or white cock, may also be part of the ritual. Worship of the *loa* is directed by the priests and priestesses of the cult, known in Haiti as *hungans* and *mambos* and in Trinidad as the *obeah* man.

The priesthood are spiritual advisers to their flock, and are consulted mainly for their predictions but also for spells and curses. If a Trinidadian has a run of very bad luck, for example, he may seek advice from the *obeah* man who will recommend a 'bush bath'. This is a bath containing a special mixture of herbs, believed to wash away the bad luck. (In fact, certain herbs used in the bath have an energising effect on the aura which can help attract better luck. I often use crystals and gemstones for the same purpose.) Unfortunately, not all visits to the *obeah* man produce such positive results. One distraught wife, on discovering that her husband was having an affair with a beautiful co-worker, had a curse put on her rival. The girl became mysteriously ill, having dreadful seizures similar to epileptic fits. No medical reason could be found for her condition, and as the seizures became more severe she had to be strapped to her bed to stop her from hurting herself. She eventually died in agony. My belief, however, is that we are not, generally speaking, at risk from curses or spells. The power of our own minds can harm as well as heal, and if we believe ourselves cursed we can draw bad luck or ill health to ourselves. Many of the charms and spells encountered in countries all over the world work because the intended victim is informed he or she is cursed, sometimes by the delivery of a token or 'fetish', such as a dead bird or small animal.

Nevertheless, the whole town of San Fernando was much impressed by the events which took place after the local *obeah* man was jailed for a minor offence. Each evening he would arrive home in time to have dinner and spend the night with his wife and family, while guards watched over his sleeping form locked in a prison cell.

This may have been a case of bi-location, the ability to be in two places at one time (a talent I have earnestly wished for myself on occasion!). The fact that it occurred during sleep, however, suggests astral travel, a practice I first became aware of in Trinidad. This is the experience of leaving one's body, known as out-of-body experiences (OOBEs), which many people achieve spontaneously. There are numerous reports of occurrences similar to the following: The son of a client of mine had been dozing on his bed when suddenly he seemed to be floating in the air. Looking down, he could see himself lying asleep on the bed. He opened his mouth to scream and then found himself 'drawn back down into his body'. He was in a state of shock, did not understand what was happening and thought he was dying.

Again, most occurrences of this nature happen while the subject is under a lot of emotional stress or under anaesthetic. In a famous case in the US a couple of years ago, a woman 'died' on the operating table while undergoing surgery. The surgeon said to his colleague: 'The old bag's gone', unaware that the woman had astrally projected from her body and was hovering overhead, able to see and hear everything. She went back into her body and, when she recovered, she sued the surgeon and won her case.

Many people travel astrally during their sleep, visiting other places, even other countries, and wake up remembering particularly vivid dreams. I studied all I could in Trinidad and spent months trying to project while in a conscious state but with no success. In my dreams, however, I succeeded in astrally travelling. I 'visited' Ireland and, accurately as it turned out, reported several changes I noticed in the area where we had lived.

It was in Trinidad also that I was introduced to yoga by a disciple of Paramahansa Yogananda, who wrote the excellent *Autobiography of a Yogi* (Yogananda died in the 1950s and his body has never decayed). This was an important milestone in my psychic development, as it introduced the spiritual dimension into my work. I recommend yoga and meditation as important steps in the development of talents in general, particularly psychic ones. These are the paths to inner power, enabling one to gain an inner control beneficial in every area of life.

Trinidad is steeped in myth and superstition. I noticed a large, strange-looking bruise on my leg one morning which I was sure had not been there the night before. I mentioned this in conversation to my fellow-students in the hospital dispensary, only to be told I had been bitten by a *succouyant*. According to local people, this is a type of vampire which appears as a ball of fire and sucks your blood when you are asleep. I received several more of these bites during the four years I spent in Trinidad but never met the *succouyant* face-to-face, thank goodness.

The old magic of crystals and gemstones is being re-discovered in current times (see Chapter 9). In Trinidad, Moslem children have always worn a blue bead as protection against the 'evil eye', a practice prevalent in most Moslem communities. Interestingly enough, many native American Indians wear turquoise beads for the same purpose.

So in Trinidad, as in Ireland, many strange and preternatural superstitions persist. I had heard reference to something called *la diablesse*, the she-devil, which my father believed he had encountered. As a man of science, he is a total sceptic but admits he has no rational explanation for his experience. Folklore has it that *la diablesse* is a woman dressed in white who accosts lone males in isolated places at night. Woe betide anyone who kisses her, as he will die.

My father was in the army during the war and was on solo sentry duty on a lonely bridge one night. He saw a woman approaching, dressed in flowing white robes, similar to the sari worn by the local Hindu women. As she drew near, she dropped the wrap from around her head to reveal a remarkably beautiful face. Looking down, he noticed she had two little hooves, like goat's hooves, instead of feet. He jumped up in sheer terror and pointed his rifle at her, whereupon she glided swiftly past him, turning to look at him. He was staring into the hideous face of a cackling old hag. He freely admits he ran back to the barracks as fast as his legs could carry him.

In Trinidad, bridges are believed to have a special link with the spirit world as many paranormal incidents are reported in these settings. My father had a second experience while guarding a bridge near Port of Spain, but this time there was another soldier on duty with him. They both saw an animal coming towards them over the bridge which they thought at first was a large donkey. As the creature got closer they could make out a grotesque face, unlike anything either of them had ever seen before. My father's companion raised his rifle and shot several times at the creature, which disappeared before their eyes. My father's friend was discharged from the army as a result of this incident. Psychiatric reports declared him unfit for duty as he had been 'seeing things' and had discharged his gun 'at nothing'.

Jim, another friend of my father's, told us of an experience he had while in college. One of his friends, Bob, claimed he had a spell which would help him pass his exams, and he invited Jim to accompany him to the local cemetery. At midnight they stood at the grave of one of Bob's relatives, where he read the words of the spell aloud. Suddenly the ground began to shake violently, and the earth on top of the grave started to move. A jet of white steam shot skywards from the centre of the grave, as the ground split open. Jim took to his heels in fright, leaving his friend behind. The next day he learned that Bob was in hospital suffering from pneumonia. He died within the week.

My first visit to a so-called 'haunted house' took place in Trinidad but was far from eventful. My parents had friends in whose house 'weird things' were supposed to happen, and I had been wanting to go there ever since I heard about it. The house had a warm, welcoming atmosphere and I must admit I was disappointed not to pick up any instant 'vibes'. The owners had a small, very beautiful, little table, the top of which was the polished cross-section of a plane tree. Trinidadian folklore says that the spirits of the dead live in these trees and they must never be cut down. The table was set on three legs which had metal tips. Every so often, the table would take fits of jumping up and down. The round marks made by the tips were visible, gouged deeply into the polished wood of the floor.

The fourth time we visited we sat on the verandah sipping iced drinks. Suddenly there was a tremendous crash from the back of the house like the sound of a tray of china and cutlery being dropped. We assumed that a maid had had an accident and were amazed when our hosts kept talking as though they had heard nothing. They told us that it happened all the time and that they were used to it by now. On checking the house, we found everything in place and nothing damaged.

I finally managed to see the table in action after visiting the house many times. I emerged from the bathroom one evening to see it hopping merrily up and down at the far end of the empty room. It stopped dead as I approached, so I stood watching to see if it would move again. I backed away to the other end of the room to encourage it and finally even begged it to jump but it refused to move. I never saw it again. I was lucky to see it even once, as many spirits are shy of performing for visitors.

The next experience I had involved a house in the residents' compound of a major oil company. Some friends of ours lived opposite a house no family had stayed in for more than two nights. They would find all their possessions strewn around the garden and the furniture turned upside down. Many had woken from their sleep in the middle of the night to find themselves being thrown out of bed. Two weeks before, the most recent tenants had woken up in the morning to find themselves lying on the front lawn, covered by their bedcovers.

I was determined to have a look at this house and got my chance a few months later when I attended a party at another house in the compound. I persuaded two friends of mine, young Scotsmen in the oil industry who were game for anything, to accompany me. We peered excitedly through the windows but saw no signs of anything unusual. We went around to the back of the house and discovered a small window open. I was slim enough to be pushed through, my hands stretched in front of me like a diver. I ended up in a heap on the pantry floor and went to let the boys in. It was pitch-black in the house, but we didn't dare put the lights on and used a torch sparingly instead. Cautiously we made our way from room to room but saw nothing unusual, just a well-furnished house that somehow didn't feel empty. The neighbours had remarked that the house always seemed occupied even though it was almost always empty.

At the doorway of one bedroom, I stopped. It seemed as if an invisible barrier was preventing me from entering. My stomach felt nauseous and waves of mingled rage and pain hit me. Instinctively I tried to communicate with whatever it was. I spoke to it in my head, saying soothing things the way I would to a frightened child or animal. This went on for about five minutes and I felt absolutely no response. Then I heard a double sigh, which faded away, and suddenly the bad feeling was gone and I was trembling uncontrollably.

My friends grabbed an arm each and ran, half carrying me, back to the sound of a steel band and a glass of rum punch (a very welcome spirit on that occasion!). I came back to Ireland not long after that and, when I returned to Trinidad eight years later, the house had been lived in for several years with no incidents. I felt intuitively that somehow I had helped the tortured soul that resided there and ever since I have been researching and developing methods for healing spirits trapped between two worlds.

When we had been in Trinidad two years, we moved to a house in Vistabella, a beautiful suburb of San Fernando. After we had been there three months, it became apparent that no-one liked staying in the spare bedroom or 'back room', as we called it. We had originally given the room to the live-in maid, Tara, but after spending one night there she asked to move into another room, without giving a specific reason. I had a good friend, Janet, a teacher on Voluntary Service Overseas from England, who often stayed with me when we went to discos together. One night, when we got back to the house, she asked if she could stay in my room instead of the back room. I agreed but found it difficult to sleep, being unused to someone sleeping in the same room. I got up finally and went to sleep in the back room myself.

We had three dogs at the time, two Alsatians who guarded the front of the house and a Dobermann Pinscher named Max, who guarded the back. As I settled down to sleep, I heard a dog walk from the left-hand side of my bed, around the foot of the bed, and up the right-hand side. I assumed that Max had been accidentally locked in and felt too tired to get up and let him out. I wasn't surprised when I felt him climb up on the bed and curl up beside my legs. I reached out to pat him and got the fright of my life – there was nothing there and yet I could still feel the shape of a warm body resting against my leg! I raced back to my own room where I spent the rest of the night tossing and turning. I got up early to find Max outside as usual and nothing out-of-the-ordinary anywhere in the house.

I told the story at breakfast but everyone insisted that I'd been dreaming, so I just let the matter drop. A few months later, my brother Richard, who had been away at school in Ireland, arrived for his summer holidays and woke up on his first morning to find a huge snake curled up on the chair near his bed. Although there are a few varieties of snake in Trinidad, it is most unusual to find one in the house. Nobody could figure out how it got in as the bedroom had been thoroughly cleaned the day before. Richard did not seem comforted by the fact that it was, in fact, a harmless snake and moved in with my other brother, Alan, for the rest of his holiday.

My mother remained sceptical, laughing everything off as coincidence and imagination. However, one night she had a row with my father and, in the time-honoured tradition, took herself off to sleep in the back room. She emerged pale and shaken the next morning and said she had spent the night in mind-to-mind battle with 'something' in the room that did not want us in the house and particularly not in that room. She said she kept telling it that we would be going back to Ireland, that we were only there for a short while. All she could feel was something trying to force us to leave.

I went into the room one day when I was alone in the house, not sure myself what I planned to do. I sat down to meditate, but couldn't do it properly because a sort of awareness was impinging on my consciousness. I could sense the room holding its breath, listening – a feeling I have become very familiar with in recent years. I stayed in the room for about an hour, sending out love and healing energy, but to my disappointment there was no apparent response. No-one slept there for a long time after that but as time went on the room gradually came to be used again. A year or so later, Alan took that room for his own and I never heard of any more disturbances there.

Years later, Richard told me the background story to our unwelcome visitor. Our next-door neighbours had employed a maid several years before who had proved unsatisfactory and had been dismissed. She vowed vengeance on her former mistress, and went to the *obeah* man to put a curse on the house. Strange things happened after that and no maid would sleep in the room set aside for their use. Finally, in desperation, the woman of the house went to the *obeah* man for a spell to get rid of the spirit. It was widely believed that it simply moved next door – into our spare room. (On hearing this tale, I fervently hoped I had not sent if on to another neighbour's house!)

It is always difficult to know the strength of the healing energy one sends out. There are factors such as ill health, which can affect its strength, but most of the time healing energy is more effective than the healer imagines. Many of my healing sessions give me no indication of what kind of results I can expect, yet there can be amazing effects within a few days. Sending out healing energy always does some good for the receiver and brings healing to the healer also. This is perfect interaction – giving healing to others and receiving healing oneself in the process.

**CHAPTER 3**

# Spirit Cats and Black Dogs

IT WAS STRANGE BEING BACK in Ireland after four years in the sunny Caribbean, but I was really happy to be home again. I became fascinated by Tarot cards. I had discovered in them the means of channelling my psychic and clairvoyant energies to produce the best results. The origins of the Tarot are not known. There are many theories, a favourite one is that they originated in Egypt and were spread throughout Europe by the gypsies. My own theory, after many years of research, is that they originated in northern Italy. The earliest deck in existence comprises twenty-six cards from a deck designed by Jacquemin Gringonneur for King Charles VI of France in 1392. Based on these, the *Tarot de Marseilles* was designed. In the Middle Ages, the Church outlawed the use of the Tarot for divination (foretelling the future).

The Tarot is actually comprised of two decks – the Major Arcana and the Minor Arcana. The Major Arcana consists of twenty-two cards, numbered '0' (the Fool) and '1' to '21', while the Minor Arcana contains fifty-six cards in four suits. The Tarot is the forerunner of modern-day playing cards. The Major Arcana disappeared, leaving the four suits of the Minor Arcana. These were: Cups (corresponding to hearts in the modern pack), Wands (clubs), Pentacles (diamonds) and Swords (spades). The court cards of the Tarot differ slightly from that of the modern playing deck. The Tarot has King, Queen, Knight and Page in each suit, while the playing cards have King, Queen and Jack. The Page was dropped and the Knight became the Jack. The Fool of the Major Arcana became the Joker.

The power of the Tarot lies in its symbols, which are geometric in design, and in its colours. This combination acts like a catalyst, allowing the user to access energies in the subconscious mind. Studying the images of the cards allows information to flow into the conscious mind, which then interprets the material. The cards are a powerful tool for helping people to know themselves better and are used by many psychologists all over the world for this purpose. Their most common use is for prediction and it was this aspect of the cards that first fascinated me.

In 1977 I made my first public predictions when I was approached by Donal Corvin, a journalist with the *Sunday Independent*, one of Ireland's leading newspapers. He wanted me to predict the outcome of the general election, which was imminent. Donal was himself a complete sceptic but thought this might make a change from the usual election material that was being printed at the time. He did not want me to prejudice the outcome in any way, so we decided to run it as a blind test.

Donal made a list of ten candidates and we dealt with them one at a time. I told him to concentrate on the person he wished to ask about. I would describe the person I saw and predict how he would fare in the election. Donal was at first amazed by the information I could give him about the people in question. I had predicted the fate of three or four candidates when I suddenly became confused. I had accurately described the person whose cards I had in front of me, yet I could not see him winning or losing. I said this to Donal and was told that he had included two politicians from the North of Ireland on the list, just to see what would happen. This was the first of the two.

At this stage Donal was beginning to accept that something was happening which he hadn't believed possible. In the end, he asked me for a reading for himself, which he was very happy with. We finished the interview and it was published the following week, a full-page spread on the back page of the *Sunday Independent*. When the election results came out a few weeks later, my predictions proved accurate. After that, I was consulted as a professional by numerous politicians, although I had no intention of working in this field.

It was not long after this that I first visited Clonegal Castle in Co. Wexford. A mutual friend of the owners and myself brought me there, thinking I had a lot in common with the Robertsons. The owner of the Castle is the Rev Lawrence Durdin-Robertson, Baron Strathloch. In the previous year, Derry, as he is known to his friends, had founded the Fellowship of Isis with his sister, Olivia, and wife, Pamela.

The castle lies within the triangular area enclosed by three rivers, known as a *macha* or 'crow's foot'. An area of this nature is often the site of a matriarchal centre, a place in which an emphasis on the feminine aspects of deity is found. Clonegal Castle is indeed a matriarchal centre, as the foundation of the Fellowship of Isis there shows. Many people today are interested in the pre-Christian religions which deified women as well as men. The holy trinity in ancient Egypt consisted of Isis, the Mother Goddess, Osiris, her consort, and Horus, their son. As bearers of children and thus bearers of life, women were considered sacred and so the Goddess was the most powerful of the ancient trinity. Through the powerful rituals and mystery plays written by Olivia Robertson, visitors to the ceremonies held at the Castle learn to develop and explore the feminine 'goddess' side of their nature. Men, women and children of every race and creed flock to the castle and all find something to suit them there. The ceremonies are held to coincide with the eight nature festivals of the year and many of them have been televised and shown world-wide.

Baron Strathloch is a tall, handsome man with a gentle, caring manner, his quiet exterior hiding a razor-sharp mind and amazingly retentive memory. His sister, the Honourable Olivia Robertson, is like a bright, living flame of energy that warms the hearts of all who meet her. They complement each other beautifully, a most unusually talented pair. They are both prolific writers, having written more than thirty books between them.

The castle itself is built of local granite and quartz. Building began in 1625 and was completed five years later. In the old basement there is an ancient well, believed to date from druidic times. It is part of the Temple of Isis, which contains twelve shrines based on the signs of the zodiac. The castle was bought in 1758 by James Lesley, Bishop of Limerick. He tripped and fell one day on the part of the stair which had no banister. He had a mahogany newel-post put in at the spot to prevent further accidents, which to this day is known as the 'Bishop's post'. His ghost has been seen on many occasions in a bedroom nearby that has a four-poster bed.

As with most castles, tales of ghosts and spirits abound. I have slept many times in the guest bedroom, which also contains a four-poster bed, dating from about 1835, with a small stairs to enable one to get into bed. Many guests have experienced a tiny, ghostly hand touching them, and I had exactly the same experience but on one occasion only. On several other occasions, I was not sure whether my imagination was playing tricks on me.

One Saturday, however, I drove to the castle after a hectic day's work. It takes almost two hours to drive from my house to Clonegal, so I was quite tired when I arrived at my destination. I dined with Olivia and Derry and we chatted for a while. We all retired at about 9.30 p.m. and I read for a while before turning off the light and settling down for the night.

I was soon sleeping soundly but, at around 1 a.m., I suddenly found myself wide awake. I held my breath and listened, wondering whether I had been woken by the sound of someone moving about, but I heard nothing. I tried to settle back to sleep but it was impossible. I was wide awake and very alert. I reached out to switch on the bedside light, when suddenly I felt it. Someone tapped me on the back of my hand, very distinctly, twice. I felt the hairs on the back of my neck prickle with fear and I just managed to save the bedside lamp, which I had almost knocked over. There was nobody there when I turned on the light. I read myself to sleep again and, although I felt rather nervous at the time, it hasn't stopped me from staying there. I have received no further visits since that night. The spirit appears to be that of a young girl, and as all souls are welcome at Clonegal, dead as well as living, I made no attempt to contact my little visitor.

The grounds of the castle are very beautiful, containing many striking and unusual trees. The garden is reckoned to be the second-oldest in Ireland, and there is a wonderful herb garden which perfumes the air there every summer. The yew walk is a line of one hundred-and-twenty ancient English yew trees at the south-east side of the castle, said to have been planted by monks. On numerous occasions, different groups of visitors to the castle have caught glimpses of a group of monks walking along the path, chanting. Others have heard the chanting but have not seen anything.

Another outdoor apparition at Clonegal is the ghost of Lady Esmonde. She appears at night in the 'spy bush' at the end of the back avenue, and is said to be watching for the return of her husband. She is accompanied by a white cat and sits combing her hair in the moonlight. Lord Esmonde married Ellice (Eilís) O'Flaherty, a grand-daughter of Grace O'Malley, *Gráinne Mhaoil*, who ruled over a large part of Connaught in the time of Queen Elizabeth I. According to the laws of the time, Esmonde, being Protestant, was able to have his marriage annulled on the grounds of her being 'mere Irishry'. Their son Thomas consequently became illegitimate and the baronial title died out, as Lord Esmonde had no children by his second wife.

Since Lady Esmonde's day, there have always been white cats at Clonegal. Cats are very psychic creatures, as are many other animals. They communicate with us in a telepathic way, often sensing our moods or even anticipating them. When a pet cat dies, the owner will often catch glimpses of their 'spirit cat' lying on a favourite bed or cushion. A friend whose cat died recently has heard him purring beside her in bed several times since he died. All who experience this feel much happier afterwards. In truth, our pets are telling us in this way that they are still with us.

I have had similar experiences myself. I once had a tiny black kitten, so small he fitted in the palm of my hand. I called him Nomi (after the German singer Klaus Nomi) and he was a member of the family until we moved to Belfast in 1987. Shortly after the move he went missing and from then on we would catch glimpses of him at night eating the food we left out for him. He had gone wild, or 'feral' as it is called. Despite all our efforts to get him back, he would not come near us. I moved back to Dublin later that year, resigned to the loss of my pet. I spent Christmas in hospital after a very bad car crash on the way to Clonegal. I had a fractured skull, fractured breastbone and had almost lost my left eye (my eyebrow had to be literally stitched back together). I really love Christmas and was feeling very sorry for myself missing all the fun. Lying dozing in my bed on Christmas Eve night, I felt a weight on my chest and opened my eyes to see an outline of Nomi, squatting on my chest. He was looking intently at me as he used to in the mornings when he wanted to coax me out of bed to feed him. He started purring gently when I opened my eyes and then faded away, leaving me with a lovely warm glow. I knew then my pet had passed on but felt really happy to know he had come back to me, even if only in spirit.

My second spirit pet is Zorai, a tiny fluffy grey-and-white, part-Persian kitten we got in 1992. We had her for only six months when she was killed tragically, leaving us heartbroken. Within a matter of weeks, my daughter Tanith and I were catching glimpses of her. She appears like a little silvery streak, jumping and playing around the house.

Ireland's most famous ghost animal is certainly the large black cat frequently seen in Killakee House. The house was built in the eighteenth century and stands in the beautiful

Wicklow hills. Above it is the infamous Hell Fire Club, where young members of the nobility gathered at night to perform magical rituals. There are also stories of every kind of excess and debauchery at their meetings and the devil is said to have appeared in their midst one night and joined them in a game of cards. The Robertsons of Clonegal and I share a common ancestor in Sir Richard Parsons, one of the members.

Killakee has had many impressive visitors in its time, including Countess Markievicz, William Butler Yeats and George Russell (AE). A personal account of Killakee is given by Sheila St Clair in her books *Psychic Phenomena in Ireland* and *The Step on the Stair: Paranormal Happenings in Ireland*.

My own most recent encounter with what I think were animal spirits was in Co. Tipperary. In answer to a call for help I found myself driving to a remote part of that county with the freelance journalist Carol Butler, who was interested in writing a feature on ghosts and spirits. A young man, whom I will call Liam, had phoned me saying that the house he lived in with his sister, Honor, seemed to 'have something in it'. He thought it might be a disturbed spirit. The house had formerly been lived in by an old lady who had herself experienced some strange things there.

He and his sister had bought the house about two years before and Liam and a friend began to modernise it. Soon they started to notice strange noises, and incidents occurred for which there was no explanation. Once when Liam was working alone in the house, he got the impression that somebody else was in the living-room with him. Then he heard footsteps in the room directly above him. There was a hole in the ceiling, as it was still being worked on. Liam looked up. At the same moment some dirt fell down on top of him, as though someone had kicked it down for a joke. Thinking that a neighbouring child might have sneaked in and was playing tricks on him, Liam went upstairs. He checked all the rooms thoroughly. But there was nobody upstairs. While renovation work was in progress, footsteps were often heard on the stairs and occasional noises came from the upstairs rooms, but these were all dismissed as 'mere imagination'.

It was shortly after Liam began to live in the house that he became sure something strange was happening. He would sense a 'presence' in the room with him, and look around certain that something would materialise, but nothing did. While shaving in front of a mirror he often caught a glimpse of something behind him, but when he looked around there would be nothing there. Honor sensed a presence in the bathroom as well, and felt something blowing gently on her neck. She also felt a sensation on her neck as though something or someone was tickling her with a feather. A friend who spent the night in the house, and who had been told nothing of these strange experiences, heard footsteps walking across the landing and in the spare bedroom, but when she investigated there was nothing there.

Things finally came to a head when friends of Honor's spent the night in the house. In the morning they heard the outside doors banging although they had all been locked the night before. The doorbell began to ring, and they heard a dreadful noise like an animal howling. This went on for two-and-a-half hours before the guests left in terror. Liam and Honor went to speak to the former inhabitant, a very alert lady, who told them that she had been wakened regularly in the middle of the night by sounds of banging and of something being dragged. She often saw animals running in and out of the cupboards in her room and saw what looked like a big black dog run under her bed. Her furniture was covered in scratches, as though made by dog claws, and all her relations and friends had seen the marks. Whenever she had cut flowers in the house she would wake in the morning to find them torn apart. The electrical sockets kept coming out of the wall and constantly needed to be replaced. She told neighbours and friends about her experiences and talked to the local priest.

The phenomena in the house were becoming more frequent and varied, Liam and Honor noticed. When walking up the stairs, Liam often felt vibrations, like footsteps, following him. Honor heard what sounded like an adult crying on the stairs, and the following night her sister heard it too. Another night there was the sound of moaning on the stairs, this time heard by six people. They described it as being like 'someone trying to frighten you'. Banging and hammering noises were a daily occurrence, sometimes going on the entire day and night. Honor was in the living-room one night at 2.00 a.m. when she heard something being dragged steadily back and forth across the floor of the bedroom above her. She then heard what sounded like a metal object being dragged across bare floorboards, although the room in question is carpeted. She agreed that the sound could have been made by claws. Honor remarked that when she was alone in the house the activity seemed to be intensified, and that switching the television on seemed to trigger off bursts of electrical disturbance, such as lights dimming and flickering and even switching themselves off.

Honor told her local priest about the happenings; he turned out to be the same priest that the former inhabitant had consulted, so he accepted her story. Two priests visited the house and said a long Latin Mass, switching to English to ask for healing for the inhabitants of the house and for those who had formerly lived there. They sprinkled holy water in each of the rooms and blessed each part of the house. Things were quiet for a few days, but unfortunately the disturbances began again less than a week after their visit.

When Honor came downstairs one morning she noticed scratches on a wooden chair she was sure had been unmarked before. On one side of the seat of the chair there were three deep scratches, like marks made by an animal's claws. When she came home at lunchtime she found that scratches had also appeared on the other side of the seat.

On my visit I was examining the chair when Honor suddenly noticed a scratch underneath as well and another on the leg which she had not seen before. Immediately I touched the chair my hands became intensely hot, a sign that someone or something in the vicinity was in need of healing. Carol took some photographs of the chair, and when they were developed one of the shots showed a patch of light which the developers of the film claim was not caused in the developing of the roll – the camera was not opened at any time and the affected photo is in the middle of the roll. I have seen similar photos taken by other investigators in spirit-inhabited houses.

I performed a clearing in this house three weeks before writing this, and so far have had no reports of further disturbances from Liam or Honor.

I discovered that animal hauntings occur in other countries too, when I left Ireland again in 1981 and went to Ibiza, a popular holiday island in the Balearics. I also discovered that language difference is no barrier when communicating with or healing spirits.

I was living in the old town of Ibiza in a tiny cobbled street called Calle de La Virgen, sharing a house with a Spanish girl called Maika. The street was a lively one, full of exotic boutiques by day and trendy nightclubs at night. The house was typical of those on the island, with thick stone walls and a heavy wooden front door and whitewashed as, by law, all the houses on the island are.

The house next door was exactly the same and a young Spanish couple, called Paloma and Manuel, lived there. The first time I entered their house I was aware that a spirit occupied it too. I said nothing, however, until Paloma confided in me that she often sensed a strange atmosphere in the house when she was alone. Several times when she was in the shower she had the distinct impression that something was watching her. Manuel worked in a nightclub and was home late at the weekends, so Paloma often slept the night with us. She confessed that she found it difficult to sleep in her own house with the sensation of someone being in the room. I told her I had a little experience of these things and would try and help if she wanted me to. She agreed eagerly, as she and Manuel did not want to move out of their house, good accommodation being difficult to find in Ibiza in summer.

With her permission I took over the house for an hour one evening when Manuel was at work. I started by 'cleansing and charging' five crystals, one for each room. I first cleansed the stones by washing them with salt and water and then rising them under running water, with the intention of clearing any negative energy. I dried each one carefully and then charged them individually by placing each crystal in the palm of my left hand and covering it with my right. I closed my eyes and visualised a bright, golden healing light pouring into me through the top of my head. I pictured the light flowing down through my arms into my hands and from my hands into the stone. I sent strong love and healing feelings through my hands to each crystal in this fashion until I could feel it really hot and then I knew the stone was charged. This is the method I use all the time. I also give each stone its purpose – good health, love, promotion, money, luck or, in this case, spirit healing.

I placed a stone in each room, together with a stick of burning incense (amber, for protection) and sat upstairs in the main bedroom to meditate. I suddenly became aware of a presence in the room with me and in my head started speaking to whoever was there. I introduced myself to 'it' but got no response. I said I felt it needed healing, that I wanted to help but needed it to tell me what it was seeking. It communicated a series of thoughts and pictures, which I interpreted as follows: The spirit was that of a man who had previously lived in the house. He was waiting for someone to return, someone he loved. I told him I would help him to move on to a better place and suddenly he was gone, like switching out a light.

I felt incredibly drained and decided to try to find out more about him before proceeding any further. Paloma and Manuel were very excited by my news and Paloma ran off to ask her friend's grandmother if she knew anything about previous tenants of the house. We discovered that a young man who had lived there committed suicide about thirty years before. He had been madly in love with his wife, who had long blond hair like Paloma. While pregnant with their first child, she fell in love with someone else and left him. He drowned himself six months later, having almost drunk himself to death in the meantime. His spirit was waiting in the house, I felt, hoping that she would return to him with their child.

I went back into the house the next night, confident that I

knew how to handle the situation. I lit incense in each room and proceeded to meditate again. This time I tuned in to him almost immediately. He was there with me but didn't seem anxious to communicate. I told him that he should listen to what I had to say, that I felt his wife was in the Afterworld and that, if he moved on, I felt sure they could sort things out. I heard a faint, low sobbing then, like the sound of a heart breaking, and so I began to send him over to the other side, radiating thoughts of love and healing. The sobbing stopped and I received an image of a tall man about thirty years old, with dark hair and a small moustache. He gave me a faint smile and then he was gone.

I walked around the house in a clockwise direction, sprinkling salt (which I had also charged like the crystals) with one hand and waving a stick of incense with the other. This was to re-balance the energies of the house and form a protective circle round it. I then 'sealed' all the doorways and windows in similar fashion to prevent other wandering spirits from entering. Finally I healed the house itself and the ground it stood on. I sent a last blast of energy to my spirit friend to help him rectify matters with his wife and went next door to rejoin my friends.

Paloma noticed the difference in her house as soon as she walked in the door. It seemed more relaxed and cheerful. It was as though a cloud of gloom had lifted. She had no more frightening experiences in that house – and this time I was sure my actions had something to do with it. For the first time, the whole impact of what I was doing hit me and I realised that spirit healing was to play an important role in my life.

I began actively to search out haunted places on the island. Some friends told us of someone they knew who had a strange tale to tell. I immediately arranged to meet him and sensed straight away that he was telling the truth. Luiz was a local businessman in his late thirties. His parents had left him a *finca* or farmhouse in the southern part of the island, near Santa Eulalia. The year before, he had started to do it up to rent to tourists in the summer, but every time he sent workmen in one or other of them complained of being attacked by a 'black dog from hell'.

None of the workmen would return, so he and his seventeen-year-old son went to work on the house themselves, to prove there was nothing to be scared of. They had a look around downstairs and then went up to the bedrooms to see what the workmen had done. As they walked in the door of the second bedroom, a 'huge, black, snarling dog with eyes of fire' came rushing at them and they ran for their lives out of the house. No longer doubting the workmen, they got the local priest up to say prayers there. One brave friend of Luiz's volunteered to go in and prove there was nothing there, but the waiting crowd was treated to the sight of him galloping out of the house as fast as his legs would carry him. Since then, no-one had set foot in the *finca*.

Luiz asked me if I could help. I told him that I could not guarantee results but I would do my best. The description he had given me sounded strangely familiar, similar to the Celtic 'black dog' frequently seen in Ireland. We arranged to meet later that week. I could see he was not very confident of my success and I must admit I was a little nervous of being attacked by a fiend of some sort, but I decided I would try my hand at some veterinary spirit healing. We set off on the appointed day and within minutes we were heading up a small side road to the house.

It was a medium-sized, two-storey house, with a large

living-room downstairs. I could feel my heart thumping as we went up the stairs and hoped Luiz couldn't hear it – or my knees knocking. Then I thought of Gerry, the big Alsatian we had as a pet when I was a child, and I focused my thoughts on the positive image of this dog. We completed our tour of the house with no interruption and walked back out into the bright sunlight, blinking at its sudden glare. We looked at each other silently and then Luiz asked me if it had gone. I told him I had done nothing to send it away yet, but was willing to work on it if he would stay in the house while I did so. I was simply too scared to be left alone there.

We came back the next day and I went through the same routine as in Paloma's house. I could not sense any kind of presence in the house but my love for animals made it easy to send out healing to whatever was there. At no time had I even the faintest awareness of a spirit energy in the house, so it is possible that it had gone before I worked on it. To make sure it was really gone, I said I would sleep in the house for a week, once I had company. Luiz brought three of his friends and we had a week-long house party in that same *finca*. Luiz was delighted, declaring me to be *una bruja*, or a witch, and telling me I could stay in the house any time I wished.

I was quite puzzled by several things in this case. I could not figure out where the dog had come from. It had certainly not been there when Luiz's father was alive and he had died only months before the first sighting of the dog. Luiz's parents had a dog but it was still alive and living with Luiz. It was also the only time in Spain or in the islands that I heard of a house being haunted by a black dog. I was still not certain that I had healed it but I never heard any strange stories about it afterwards and to my knowledge the house is inhabited to this day.

As a teenager, I remember hearing a friend of my mother's describe an experience she had while on holiday in Co. Galway. Maura was a very down-to-earth, practical person, not given to over-imagination. She was cycling home down a lonely boreen on a moonlit night. Suddenly, she found the road barred by a huge black dog, with red glowing eyes. It just stood staring at her, wagging its tail slowly from side to side. Needless to say she turned her bike and cycled for dear life back to the house she had just left. There are numerous reports in Ireland concerning a black dog but I obviously tracked one down on his holidays in Ibiza.

I was very sad leaving Ibiza. I was in love with the energy of the island and the beauty of the place and its people, but Ireland drew me back home eventually, as she always does.

## CHAPTER 4

# Stephen Moves on to the Light

AFTER RETURNING TO IRELAND IN 1982, I founded the Irish Institute of Parapsychology and Metaphysics. The Institute's primary aim is to research and evaluate paranormal happenings as well as psychic talents such as telepathy, clairvoyance and remote viewing. Another ambition, which as yet remains unfulfilled, is to establish standards in the psychic field and set up a code of practice for professionals working in this area. The Institute also has other functions: to teach people how to develop their psychic and healing abilities and how to become professionals in both fields.

As part of these aims, I set up a psychic studies group of my most talented students and we met in my house once a week to discuss, develop and research our favourite subjects. We spent many hours working with everything from breathing exercises to visualisation techniques, from astral travelling to telepathy. It was then I discovered my love of teaching, something that is with me still. An interesting observation I made at that time is still influencing my work today. I noticed that, as my students developed their psychic skills, their self-confidence and self-esteem increased as well. To a certain extent, the same is true when we develop any type of talent, but I feel that channelling of psychic and healing energy is a true key to empowerment.

One of my students was a young man called Anthony. He seemed particularly interested in the paranormal and frequently asked questions about ghosts and spirits. He asked me one day if he could bring his girlfriend to see me and told me that she had been 'plagued by some kind of spirit' since childhood. This immediately aroused my interest, so he arranged to bring her to my house the following week.

Ann-Marie was eighteen, a petite, striking-looking blonde with eyes that seemed to see far-away things. Apart from her unusual energy, the first thing I noticed about her was her strong talent as a medium. I had no doubt that she could see spirits and began to question her about her experiences. At first she seemed embarrassed to talk about them, starting each sentence with 'This probably sounds mad, but …' or 'I know this sounds crazy …'. However, she began to relax a little when she realised that I was taking what she told me seriously. We talked long into that first night.

From early childhood, Ann-Marie had had a constant companion who no-one else could see. From her description he was not the standard 'imaginary friend', which many children have. She described him as a dark-haired, pale-faced man who looked to be in his twenties. Everywhere she went as a child he was there watching her, sometimes making faces at her but mostly just watching. When she went to bed at night he would sit on the side of her bed and pull her hair and tickle her, pull at the bedclothes and generally make it impossible for her to sleep for more than a few minutes. As soon as she fell asleep, he would wake her up again. She felt that he did not want her to go asleep at all. When she reached puberty the situation became much worse. She experienced frequent slaps in the face and was thrown heavily out of her bed on numerous occasions.

Early one morning, both she and one of her sisters were flung from their beds in this fashion, and the two beds rose up in the air before the horrified eyes of the girls and crashed through the bedroom window. Ann-Marie's parents and a group of curious neighbours had already gathered around the beds on the front lawn by the time the girls plucked up the courage to look out the window. This incident was reported in the local newspapers at the time, yet Ann-Marie's attempts to explain her plight were still ignored by those she tried to talk to.

Another night she was lying in bed when she was suddenly flung violently against the bedroom wall and had bruises on her side and shoulder from the impact. On still another occasion, she sprained her wrist as she was pulled out onto the floor. Most of these incidents happened in full view of at least one other member of her family but no-one else could see 'him'. In some way the family appeared to be blaming Ann-Marie for the odd happenings in the house, as though somehow she were making them happen.

After the 'flying bed' incident her parents sent her to talk to a priest, which was the closest they ever came to admitting that there was a problem. The priest listened with sympathy to her tale, interrupting her now and then to ask questions. When she had finished her story, his assessment of the case was that she was suffering from an over-active imagination. 'There are no such things as ghosts,' he informed her kindly but firmly. He recommended certain religious books and prayers, telling her that was all the advice he could offer her.

Nobody had ever believed Ann-Marie's story before she met me. She had lived in a state of intense anxiety and tension all her life. Some of this stress came from her feeling of isolation. Her parents and siblings did not know what to make of her story. Like many Irish families, they belonged to the 'ignore it and it will go away' school of thought and were inclined to believe that she was 'looking for attention'. Consequently, she had withdrawn a little into herself and found it difficult to trust easily. We got on very well together so I invited her to join our weekly group to develop her own inner resources to help in this situation.

We began working together regularly. I felt my immediate task was to help her rebuild some of the self-confidence and self-esteem which had suffered dreadfully because of her situation. This involved teaching her first how to develop her own inner psychic energies. In the class, I began to instruct my students in ways of developing the right-hand side of the brain. These included basic techniques like using the left hand more for writing, ironing, painting – anything that develops and strengthens the left hand. (A great many left-handed people are very psychic because using the left hand physically develops the intuitive right-hand side of the brain. I myself have been ambidextrous since childhood.) Another method for integrating the two sides of the brain involves drawing a figure '8', over and over again using the left hand. A more enjoyable exercise is to use chopsticks when eating. It was interesting to note that, in the regular telepathy testing sessions with the group, each member's accuracy rating was seen to improve as the weeks went on.

During our first meeting, Ann-Marie had told me that her sleep pattern was badly affected by her experiences. Even

## Stephen Moves on to the Light

when she did manage to sleep, she would wake up after a few hours, either woken by 'him' or by her bad dreams. She was having a lot of nightmares and was living in fear of either waking or sleeping. To help deal with these nightmares, I decided to begin some dream work with the class, a subject in which they were all interested. Our exercises focused on 'lucid dreaming', i.e. where the dreamer is able to exert conscious control over dream material, and to wake at will when having a nightmare. Many people experience this spontaneously by being aware, on occasion, that they are dreaming *when* they dream. This concept first appeared among the Tibetan yogis, and is explored in the American dream laboratories to this day.

To induce lucid dreaming takes time and effort, but can provide a solution to frightening or troublesome dreams. I suggest a lavender bath and some deep breathing exercises to induce relaxation. Programme a quartz crystal by charging it (see Chapter 3), saying the words 'I will control my dreams' several times. Place the crystal next to your bed or under the pillow. Tell yourself you will practise controlling your dreams this night while you sleep. Eventually you will be able to exert dream control at will, and change the course of action of the dream. You can also wake yourself up at will if necessary.

Many of Ann-Marie's bad dreams were not of spirit origin but were her subconscious replaying negative experiences. In two or three months she had gained enough dream control to wake herself up when frightened. These exercises helped Ann-Marie to know herself more fully as well as to resolve a lot of her own inner conflict by exploring dream symbolism.

I also taught Ann-Marie the techniques for psychic self-defence, in order to help her experience her own inner strength before I worked on the troublesome spirit plaguing her. I suggested she light some amber incense and practise some deep breathing exercises. One powerful technique I call the 'golden balloon' involves sitting in a comfortable position with the spine held straight. Start some slow, deep breathing, telling yourself to relax. With every in-breath picture yourself breathing in bright, golden light. With every out-breath feel yourself breathe away all your aches and pains, stresses and tensions, troubles and worries. When you are feeling relaxed, imagine you are sitting inside a giant balloon which lies loosely around you. As you breathe in, visualise the bright, golden light pouring through the top of your head, energising you. As you exhale, breathe out bright, golden light which gradually begins to fill the balloon around you. Continue breathing and visualising until the balloon is stretched and taut, filled with golden light. Enjoy and absorb the golden energy for a while. Now focus your eyes on your solar plexus (above the waist, between your ribs) and picture a bright, white light beginning to form there. Visualise this light moving to your right to form the beginning of a circle. Picture this light travelling around the back of your body to join itself at the solar plexus, forming a ring. See yourself surrounded by this glowing white circle, holding the image until it begins to fade. Gradually return your breathing to normal. This is known as a 'protective circle', and you may place it around others as well as yourself.

Ann-Marie soon became more confident through her work with the group and gained acceptance in a way she had not experienced before. Instead of being thought of as 'weird' or 'odd' because of her experiences, she found herself the centre of an admiring company of psychic enthusiasts. She was questioned avidly about every aspect of the situation and, after years of negative reactions to her story, found valuable healing in the acceptance and positive feedback of her companions. For the first time, I became aware of how powerful the healing influence of a group could be.

In tackling this case, I must admit I was quite apprehensive although, for Ann-Marie's sake, I acted as though I dealt with this sort of thing on a regular basis. The truth of the matter was that I had never encountered anything quite like this before. I was worried that either Ann-Marie or I or both of us would be hurt if 'he' objected to what I would try to do. Because I had never dealt with a case of this nature, I was afraid I might encounter something I was unprepared to deal with. I have never heard personally of anyone who has been damaged physically or emotionally by a spirit. Many old ghost stories, however, mention people dying or becoming insane or having their hair turn snow white as a result of spirit encounters. If Ann-Marie's spirit could throw beds out of a window, I reasoned, then maybe he could do the same with human beings. So I decided to wait until Ann-Marie was sufficiently energised by her work in the group and with me while, at the same time, I worked on some absent healing.

After a short time, Ann-Marie was responding very well to healing and the psychic exercises. We also noticed that things had quietened down since I had started using visualisation therapy (see Chapter 7) on her tormentor. The techniques I had taught her to control her dream content were also working so we set a date to begin the healing process. I invited Ann-Marie to stay at my house, as I wanted to keep her near me in case of any unexpected developments.

On the appointed day, I sent my daughter Tanith to a friend's house to spend the night and her father decided to go with her 'in case she got scared during the night'. I teased him about being frightened himself but he denied it, leaving the house with that strained look and uncertain smile of a man pretending not to be fearful.

There was a strange atmosphere in my house that day, the 'phone scarcely rang (a blessing, it usually never stops). I had no visitors. Even the cats were reluctant to stay in the house and vanished the minute they were let out, not even bothering to come back for dinner. I'm sure I was emitting some strange energy as I really was worried for Ann-Marie. Also the question kept nagging at the back of my mind: Is 'he' stronger than me?

The only people staying in my house that night would be myself, Ann-Marie and Anthony, who had gallantly insisted on joining us. Of course, the entire study group had wanted to stay as well to witness what went on. I had to be quite firm and explain that I could not take chances with a situation like this and that two people were enough to be responsible for.

We had held a group healing circle in preparation the night before and the questions asked by the others were still ringing in my ears: 'What if it goes berserk and kills Ann-Marie or even all three of you? Your hair will probably go white! Maybe it's the devil!' (As I mentioned earlier, the group can be a great source of healing and comfort!)

To be honest, I was feeling quite nervous as the time drew closer. The three of us began a meditation to help us relax and practised psychic self-defence techniques to strengthen and protect ourselves. We then adjourned to the reading room, which I had decided was most appropriate for the task in hand. This is the room in which I do all my work. In every house I've ever lived in, there has been some room called by that name, as most of my work is reading Tarot. All my spiritual and healing work is done there and one gets a perceptible build-up of positive energy in such a room. In fact, it becomes a 'power room' because it can empower you and re-balance your energies when you find yourself in a state of disharmony. As soon as I walked through the door that evening I felt my apprehensions disappear.

My two companions and I sat comfortably on the floor on bean bags and began to meditate. I then began a guided visualisation with Ann-Marie, leading her into a light trance where I felt she would be more relaxed. I brought her back to her childhood, regressing her to the time when she had first set eyes on 'him'. Intuitively I felt that, as the violent attacks had begun when she reached puberty, he might be easier to deal with if I brought her back to childhood. When I had brought her back to the age of seven, I asked her to call him, to tell him someone wanted to talk to him. Immediately the door of the room burst open as though blown open by a strong wind, but strangely Ann-Marie did not seem to hear it. Anthony, on the other hand, leaped approximately two feet into the air in fright but closed the door with a shame-faced look when he saw neither Ann-Marie nor I had reacted.

I suggested to Ann-Marie that she ask the spirit his name and she told me he called himself 'Stephen'. I held her hand and told her to tell him I wished to speak with him, that I would like to help him. I invited him to come and join us and suddenly became aware of him, smiling slyly at me like a shy little boy. He seemed to be pleased with our invitation and he sat beside us on the floor, joining our circle. I told him I could send him 'home' to a safe secure place where he belonged but he indicated that his home was with Ann-Marie, wherever she was. He did not seem to understand the concept of 'safe' and I gathered that he could not ever remember having a 'home' while he was still alive, but had lived as a vagrant all his life.

I discovered that his responses varied with our attitudes. While I questioned him gently and caringly, he responded civilly enough, although I must admit his strange, lopsided leer was rather disconcerting and I could see that his appearance frightened Ann-Marie. At one stage he reached out a hand to touch her hair and she recoiled in horror, so he slapped her hard across the ear. I steeled myself not to react in a negative way and, putting my arms around Ann-Marie, said: 'Don't be upset, Stephen just wants to touch your beautiful hair,' and was very relieved to see him nodding vigorously.

I felt then that he really liked Ann-Marie and was reacting with violence to her rejection of him, so I started working on him to move on, assuring him that, if he did, Ann-Marie would be his friend for all eternity. He disappeared suddenly, and I was left talking to myself.

'Call him back, tell him you care about him,' I told Ann-Marie and suggested that she get ready to give him a big, loving smile on my signal. She called him back and he reappeared, sitting right beside her on her bean bag, staring into her face. 'Stephen,' I said to him. 'Ann-Marie and I want you to move on. Ann-Marie cares about you, she wants you to be happy. If you move forward into the light, Ann-Marie will be happy for you. She will love you always.'

As I spoke, I was pouring out golden healing light to this poor creature who, I was sure, had never felt love or happiness in his life. 'You make Ann-Marie afraid when you visit her on this earth in the way you do. Do you want her to love you?' He turned dark, tormented eyes in my direction and for the first time we made eye contact. There was an almost electrical energy about his eyes, which seemed composed of glittering

## Stephen Moves on to the Light

lights that shifted and changed. He nodded slowly, emphatically, and the look in his eyes appeared now like a dumb appeal. I heard his question clearly in my mind: How?

I turned to look at Ann-Marie who, I was happy to see, seemed alert and composed. 'If you want Ann-Marie to love you,' I said casually, 'you'll have to do what she asks you. You know how stubborn women can be.' My mad sense of humour had broken through once more at precisely the wrong time, I thought, only to notice him watching the girl with a grin in place of his usual leering expression. 'Ann-Marie wants you to move on to your proper spirit home,' I continued. 'It makes her unhappy to see you here on earth. It frightens and upsets her when you get angry with her. If you move on, you will still be able to see her, you know. You yourself will feel great peace and happiness and you will see Ann-Marie looking better and happier than ever before.' I got the impression he was enjoying all the attention as he listened intently but gave no indication of how he was taking my words.

I was beginning to feel a little tired at this stage so I took a deep breath and tried again. 'Ann-Marie wants you to move on to the light. She will send you loving thoughts every day if you move on. Isn't that right, Ann-Marie? Tell him.'

Anthony, face chalk-white, reached for her hand but she ignored it, shaking her head. I felt that she sensed, as I had, that Stephen might be jealous of Anthony if he saw any signs of affection between them.

Ann-Marie's voice was surprisingly calm and controlled when she spoke. 'Stephen, I want you to go to the light, where you belong. I will send you healing thoughts of love every day.' Ann-Marie was smiling at him, a bright, genuine smile that caused Anthony and me to glance at each other in amazement.

I think we were both proud of her at the moment, she was handling this so well. Stephen left so suddenly, it made us jump. One minute he was sitting smiling at the pale, blond girl sitting beside him: the next he was gone. There was an emptiness in the room that was almost tangible, a strange vacuum. I felt my eyes prickle with tiredness and my back begin to ache. 'Let's make a cup of coffee,' I said. 'I think he's gone.'

I looked at my watch as we headed for the kitchen and remarked that I thought we had been hours in meditation whereas, in fact, we had been thirty-five minutes. At first we thought my watch must have stopped but it proved to be correct. We all felt shaken, disoriented, with a distinct feeling of anti-climax. I knew Stephen had gone. Ann-Marie seemed sure of it too – but Anthony was not convinced.

'I'll know for sure when I go to bed,' said Ann-Marie, who looked pale but relaxed. We talked for a while and then made ourselves something to eat. We decided to get an early night as everyone was exhausted and we knew we would feel better when we had got the night over.

I was so drained I fell asleep immediately and passed an undisturbed night. In the morning I was up before Ann-Marie and sent her a blast of healing as she lay sleeping peacefully. When she woke up, she told me that Stephen had said his goodbye to her just as she was drifting off to sleep the night before. 'I felt a puff of air on my cheek, like someone gently blowing on me. I half-opened my eyes and I saw his face, smiling at me. Then I fell asleep.'

That was in February 1984. I spoke to Ann-Marie last year and she has never had any contact from Stephen since.

**CHAPTER 5**

# The World of the Spirit

THE HUMAN PSYCHE is a strange, beautiful and complex thing, both in life and in death. In the normal course of events, when we die we move on to the realm of spirit where we are not normally accessible to communication to or from those still living. But some souls do not move on in the usual way and become 'earthbound'. They are, in effect, trapped between two worlds – that of the living and that of the dead.

Many aspects of the human condition still escape our understanding. Why for example, does a young man go berserk and slaughter his family? Or kill and eat fellow human beings? We have all read of similar horrors. In the same way, it is impossible to explain exactly why many should linger in their former homes making their presence felt and alarming the current inhabitants. Probable explanations include the possibility that some souls do not realise they have died. Others remain frozen in a state of psychic shock because of a violent or sudden death. Still others may be too connected to this earth and its inhabitants to move on peacefully. Whatever the reason, it is impossible to deny the existence of spirit activity. Cases have been recorded since the beginning of time and examples occur all over the world on a daily basis. We tend to refer to these phenomena as ghosts but, in fact, there is a definable difference between these experiences.

## SPIRITS

In *Chambers Dictionary,* the word 'spirit' has many definitions including vital principle; the soul; a disembodied soul; a ghost; an incorporeal being. Spirit is then, in a sense, the essence of a person, living or dead. It is often used as a blanket term, covering different types of paranormal phenomena such as ghosts, poltergeists and apparitions. Yet to the professional ghost buster, there are differences between spirits and other phenomena.

A spirit retains a personality and is capable of independent thought and action, while a ghost appears two-dimensional by comparison. Spirits interact and communicate with the living and can move from place to place. They account for the majority of the minor phenomena reported so frequently and most of them are connected with a particular piece of land or a house. On almost a daily basis I hear tales of random footsteps, doors opening or banging, presences being felt in various rooms. These are genuine spirit phenomena, although usually so mild that the residents in such houses don't do anything about them. I have also encountered incidents of 'personal spirits' who become attached to particular people and follow them from place to place, even from country to country.

An early contact I had with this sort of case was in the late 1970s in the Sandymount area of Dublin. I was at a party with a friend – I'll call her Anna – and we were sitting together on a

## The World of the Spirit

couch facing a large mirror on the wall in front of us. In the mirror I noticed a young man leaning on the couch behind us, apparently listening to our conversation. I turned around and there was no-one behind me, but when I turned back he was still clearly visible in the mirror, resting his elbow on the back of the couch. He had shoulder-length black hair with a beard and moustache and wore a dark red, floppy hat – regulation hippy garb of the era. Again I turned around quickly, even looking down behind the couch to see if he was hiding there, but there was no sign of him in the room.

As I was describing to Anna what I had seen, she said: 'Oh, that sounds exactly like my Cavalier,' and I realised that was precisely what he had reminded me of. She said that for several years she had been catching glimpses of this young man, mostly at home, but sometimes in other houses and once standing behind her in a queue at the bus-stop. She described him exactly as I had seen him, down to the colour of his hat. He was extremely handsome and I thought at the time it was just my luck to meet such a gorgeous ghost only to find he was already 'taken'.

It often happens that the spirit haunting a house is that of a suicide. One day I got a message to 'Phone Liz urgently'. Liz, it turned out, lives in a modern, semi-detached house on the northside of Dublin. She told me that the smallest of her bedrooms was always icy cold and that the door could only be kept closed by locking it. Neither of her teenage daughters would sleep in the room as they would have nightmares and wake up several times during the night, crying and frightened. When I visited the house I realised that both mother and daughters had mediumistic abilities, in fact, Liz was taking a course in healing. They accompanied me upstairs and unlocked the door of the bedroom. Immediately, I felt the cold atmosphere and sensed a spirit presence. Liz said she had twice heard someone walking across the room when she was in the house alone. Deirdre, the younger daughter, had heard footsteps on the landing several times; and Maeve, the older daughter, frequently had the feeling she was being watched as she walked across the landing to her room. On one occasion, when she was coming home from school, she glanced up at the window of the bedroom and was convinced she saw an old woman looking down at her.

I set to work to try to rid the room of its unwelcome guest. With surprising ease I tuned into a small, gaunt-faced woman in her fifties who stared at me with pain-filled brown eyes. A remarkable story unfolded in my mind. She had lived, I felt, in a house on the same spot around the turn of the century, the only daughter of a well-to-do family. She had been seduced by her father's brother and had borne a child by him. The family had gone to great lengths to conceal her pregnancy, keeping her locked in a small room, and taking the child away once it was born. They refused to tell her anything about the child and she believed they had killed it. She lived as a recluse for the rest of her life and finally hanged herself, ending her miserable existence.

I sent her love and healing, telling her I could help her pass into the Afterworld where she could experience love and light. I worked on her for nearly an hour. She did not deliberately resist me in any way, but her extreme sadness seemed to place a wall around her and I had to work hard to break it down. Finally I heard the sound of sobbing and I felt her let go and pass over, still crying. When I went downstairs I found Liz and her daughters huddled together, looking very agitated. They had heard the sound of crying from upstairs and were terrified. I reassured them that to the best of my knowledge the room was now cleared. I made coffee and tea and started to work on the living, asking Liz to help me as I turned to the girls and showed them how to experience their own healing abilities. Soon things were back to normal. As a final precaution, I re-balanced the energies in the house. They have used the room many times since then with no problems.

One Halloween I received a cry for help from the Ashbourne area in Co. Meath, where a friend of mine lives in a secluded house deep in the countryside. He wanted me to meet his only neighbours, who I will call Marjorie and David. Their house was built by David's family about one hundred-and-fifty years ago on the site of a much older house which had also been lived in by his family. David told me that since his childhood he had been aware that the house was said to be haunted and that incidents had occurred which had no explanations. He himself twice saw a tall figure, which he took to be male, clad in a long dark-coloured cloak there. The first time he was seven years old and the figure was in the library standing with his back to him, looking out the window. The child asked: 'Who are you?' and the figure vanished before his eyes. Then on his eleventh birthday, David saw the figure again in the hallway below him as he descended the stairs. Leaning over the banister, he called to the figure, but it seemed to melt into the wall near the front door.

Over the years members of David's family had often heard heavy footsteps on the stairs, when nobody was there; sounds of fighting were frequently reported at night below one of the bedroom windows; doors seemed to open and close by themselves from time to time. These incidents were dismissed as being just a feature of the age of the house.

But one night David's daughter Jill had been badly frightened, and this caused her parents to take action and ask me to see the house. She had slept in the guest bedroom because the heating in her own room was faulty. The sound of loud voices woke her up, then she heard the sound of steel striking steel 'like a sword fight'. She sat up, leaned over to turn on the lamp and as she did so the bedroom door opened with a crash and she saw a large black figure with a vague, featureless face, looking at her. Her screams brought her parents to her side, and when David checked below the window, and later over the grounds, nothing unusual was detected. If any living person had looked in Jill's door that night he would have had to pass by David, who ran out on the landing immediately, or else jump a huge drop to the hall below.

Although normally a down-to-earth and outgoing girl, Jill was very disturbed by the incident. She was home on holiday from London were she was studying music, and for the rest of her stay she became preoccupied and jumpy. She was intent on finding a logical explanation for the event, examining locks on the upstairs windows, which had all been found to be locked securely on the night in question. Her parents were anxious to ensure that their only child would not have any further unpleasant experiences in their home.

I reached the house early on a Saturday morning and set to work at once. It was a bright and sunny November day and I began outdoors. First, I set about healing the land immediately around the house, paying particular attention to the area under the guest-bedroom window. This area felt noticeably colder to me than the other side of the house which was in shadow at the time. I sat on the ground, right in the centre of the 'cold spot' and put myself into a light trance. I tried to tune in to the spot and see what had happened there in the past to cause the problems. To my disappointment the only images that arose were of six or seven grey-clad men on horseback. I spent twenty minutes in all meditating there, but no further information was forthcoming. I began to send bright, golden healing light down deep into the earth. Then I sent out golden rays in a circle all around me, healing the land as far as I could see. This took about another half-hour, and then I felt a familiar wrench at my solar plexus and that light-headed, almost giddy, feeling I get when there is nothing left to heal. Stiff and cold, I headed indoors for a much-needed cup of coffee.

My next task was to prepare crystals for distribution around the house, so I cleansed and charged the stones and placed them in each of the rooms. I then treated a beeswax candle with amber oil (for protection) and left it burning in the guest bedroom. I began to meditate in that room and attempted to make contact with the troubled spirit. I started to shake violently and sensed anger and aggression like a dark cloud around me. I began to send out healing to whatever was there although no real contact had been made, and I set about filling the room with golden light. The dark cloud, which was almost visible and tangible, gradually evaporated until the atmosphere in the room felt peaceful and positive, and I sank back in my chair, drained.

I took another break, showered and lay down for half-an-hour before lunch. After a delicious meal I felt energised enough to work around the rooms with salt and amber incense. I performed a healing meditation in two of the other bedrooms which felt as though they needed it, and decided to treat the rest of the house on the following day. I had chosen to sleep in the guest bedroom that night and, indeed, I felt a little apprehensive. Although I was exhausted both mentally and physically it took me at least two hours to read myself to sleep, and I persuaded myself that I did not feel nervous. I was almost disappointed to wake up to bright sunlight and croissants and coffee, having slept soundly all night!

Next day I meditated and sent out healing in all the other rooms of the house. My intuition told me it would be a good idea to do some more work in the guest bedroom, so I spent another fifteen minutes or so there. The whole clearing felt like something of an anticlimax, but I was confident there was nothing left in the house to bother David's family again. I kept in touch with them for almost three years and they had no further unwelcome visitors from the other side.

## APPARITIONS

An apparition is a vision or sighting of a person either living or dead. Apparitions of those who have passed on are usually experienced as ghosts or hauntings (see below). Many reports world-wide tell of point-of-death apparitions. A client of mine from Co. Cork gave me this story. She had been asleep for about two hours when suddenly she found herself wide awake. The clock said 1.20 a.m. and she turned to settle herself in the bed. Then she saw her husband sitting in the chair at the foot of the bed, looking towards the floor. 'I thought he'd lost his job or had an accident. I remember praying that he hadn't killed someone with the truck, he looked so miserable.'

Her husband was a truckdriver who should have been in Northern Ireland, three hundred miles away. 'I asked him what was wrong and he looked up and smiled at me. Then he disappeared before my very eyes.' Less than an hour later came the 'phone call telling her that her husband had died of a heart attack at 1.20 a.m. As his soul left his body, this man had somehow projected an image of himself home to his wife, seemingly to bid her farewell.

There are hundreds of reports of similar incidents, which happen, I feel, spontaneously rather than deliberately. I have also come across cases where the person seen is actually living. Again, these usually happen at times when either party is in a state of acute distress. I myself had such an experience, unusual because I had no prior connection with the other party involved. I was renting a house in Killiney, Co. Dublin, and knew nothing about the owners except that they lived abroad. It was a bright summer day in June 1984, and I was going upstairs to my bedroom. While walking across the landing I glanced into the bathroom and saw a blond lady in her thirties leaning into the bath as if to fill or clean it. She was dressed in modern clothing and looked solid and real. As I looked, she disappeared. Four months later the lease on the house expired and on the day I was leaving I came face to face with the same woman. She and her husband were the owners of the house, and were back now and ready to move into it after several years abroad. Several months later, I learned that she had been extremely homesick and had suffered a miscarriage weeks before I saw her in the bathroom.

## GHOSTS

Ghosts may be sensed, heard or seen in a particular spot connected with them while they were living. Often some form of tragedy such as suicide caused the actual death. Many descriptions of ghost encounters portray a semi-transparent, gliding form. But many ghosts are not seen at all. They may be heard or sensed as an invisible presence. They rarely travel or move from their usual place, although occasionally 'house ghosts' have been spotted in the garden.

Ghosts do not throw things about or play practical jokes. Neither do they display the type of intelligence often displayed by poltergeists. Apparently incapable of reasoning, they seem locked into a sad replay of some significant event or time, going through the motions in a mechanical way. People with a developed psychic ability are more likely to experience a ghost but the majority of reports come from individuals apparently undeveloped in this area. Much of my own work involves working with a person's energies, helping to re-align and re-balance them through various forms of healing. So in a sense, it was a logical progression for me to heal and balance the energies of those who have passed on. Ghosts are a form of trapped energy absorbed by a place or building, the personality of a person living on in the half-world between this and the next.

Many old buildings contain a resident ghost, but I met a 'modern' ghost in a six-year-old house in Greystones, Co. Wickow. A friend, Ronan McKenna, who is very psychic contacted me: he had been approached by someone looking for my help. Ronan brought me to the house and asked if he could stay and see what happened. As soon as we entered the kitchen, he declared that he could 'feel something, a presence' which confirmed what I felt.

On two occasions, Tina, who lived in the house, had walked into the kitchen to see a 'small woman kneeling on the floor, scrubbing or cleaning it'. The first time Tina saw it was about a year after she and her boyfriend moved in. She had put it down to imagination or overwork and had forgotten the incident until a year or so later when it happened again. As she stared in amazement the figure started to fade, and vanished into thin air. Tina described the woman as looking about seventy years old, with her hair in a bun and wearing a brown overall. She seemed not to have noticed Tina at all but was totally absorbed in her task. These were the only two incidents she had to relate so I presumed I was dealing with a ghost in this case, rather than a noisy poltergeist or personal apparition. I could not establish a full link with my 'busy ghost', although I did catch a glimpse of her fading backwards through the wall as I worked. To my knowledge she has never visited Tina since.

Objects too can have their associations which may become disturbed and the spirits 'reactivated'. One case like this occurred in Dublin in a house built alongside one of the canals. A young couple, Joan and John, had bought a small stone cottage there after its elderly resident had gone to a nursing home. They set about refurbishing it, and behind a brick in the wall found an old leather pouch containing three pieces of polished jet (a black stone popular during Victorian times in jewellery, especially in mourning jewellery) and two black feathers. They presumed this was some sort of charm, to bring good luck to the household, perhaps.

The night after the discovery of the pouch, Joan woke up at 2.00 a.m. with the distinct feeling that there was someone in the room. Hearing a muffled thud in the corner, she woke John. He got up and put on the light, but everything seemed normal. They talked for ten minutes or so, listening for any further sounds, then switched off the light and settled down to sleep again. Just as John was dozing off a loud rap on the wall next to the bed made Joan scream. John leapt out of bed and put on the light again. There was still nothing to be seen, but this time they were both certain they had experienced something. When they calmed down, and nothing further happened, they decided to go downstairs and make a cup of tea. They were both terrified, shaking as they descended the stairs, and they looked for logical reasons for the noises. As Joan poured the tea, they heard a loud crash from upstairs. Joan dropped the teapot, and they ran for the front door, grabbing the car keys as they left. They drove straight to Joan's mother's house and roused the household with their story. They were not prepared to go back to the house until I could arrange to go with them, so I agreed to go the following day.

They both took the day off work, and I met them at the cottage at 10.00 a.m. Holding hands, the two crept nervously into the house behind me. Everything seemed quite normal except for the teapot on the floor, which Joan soon filled with steaming tea. We had a cup together while we chatted before going up to the bedroom. They were both apprehensive, but when we went upstairs, however, there was nothing out of place and I could tell by John's face that he was beginning to feel a bit foolish. My own assessment was that there was, in fact, a spirit presence in the house.

I suggested that the couple wait in a nearby pub while I worked on the room, and said I would join them when I had finished. I worked on the land around the cottage, then proceeded to work on the bedroom. I found myself tuned into a male presence, but the link was very faint. I sent out healing and had no sense of reaction from the spirit, but I just kept on projecting golden light. A thought formed unbidden in my mind: Put the charm back. It repeated itself over and over in my head, and then I realised I had lost the link with the spirit. I could sense that the presence was still there and I tried to make contact with it again. But only the thought: Put the charm back, kept coming into my mind.

I went to the pub and brought Joan and John back into their home, telling them of my experience. Joan said immediately to John: 'I knew that was what we would have to do, I told you,' and John agreed that this was what she had said in the pub. I examined the objects from the pouch, psychometrising them. This involves absorbing feelings from an object to receive memories associated with it (see Chapter 10 for exercises to develop this technique). I felt that the feathers came from a woman's hat and the stones from a bracelet belonging to the same person. My impressions were that they were mementos of a dead wife, hidden in the wall for good luck by her loving husband. I put them back in the pouch, sent healing energy into them, charging them to emit positive energy from their hiding place. We replaced them behind the brick, sealing the opening with plaster. I can honestly admit that this was the only case where my skills as a plasterer were called into play!

I went on to re-balance the energies in the house and then worked on John and Joan. I was pleased to see that they both looked a lot happier, but they confessed to a reluctance to spending the night in the house alone. I telephoned home to make arrangements for my children and offered to spend the night in their room while they slept in the other bedroom. We all passed a very peaceful night. They were still reluctant to spend the night alone so we came up with a list of relations and friends who might come to stay. For the next three weeks people stayed with them until they finally felt safe enough to return to normal living. They have had no further problems in their home.

## POLTERGEISTS

Poltergeist is the German term for a 'noisy spirit', though the Germans themselves prefer to call it a 'Spuk'. Most of the cases I have been called in to investigate in Ireland have involved this type of spirit. Commonly reported phenomena include rappings, banging or dragging noises, objects moving mysteriously through the air or from one place to another, furniture and household objects being rearranged in full view of onlookers. In the earlier days of psychic research, most of the cases investigated involved a teenager, usually female, living in the house. It was widely believed that this young person somehow 'caused' the disturbances. The energies of teenagers at puberty are quite different from those of most adults, in the same way that the energies of a schizophrenic differ from those of others. The presence of a teenager in the house can act as a magnet to a wandering spirit. In the majority of reports – though it is not an essential factor in all – this proves to be the case.

Usually, a specific person, possessing strong psychic or mediumistic energies, is the central focus for what we now call polterkinetic activity. The person involved is not aware of this nor to blame in any way. Poltergeists seem to have a sense of humour as they frequently play practical jokes. They do not harm or hurt people and are often referred to as 'playful ghosts'. Some of them actually form a sort of relationship with the family concerned or with certain members of it, as a recent case I dealt with shows.

Donal lives with his wife Eileen and their three children in a cottage near Wicklow town. He told me that everyday, objects in the house were moved from place to place, and even from room to room. On one recent occasion, the whole family watched with alarm as a teacup slid down the length of the

## The World of the Spirit

kitchen table. Sometimes they were woken up in the night by the sound of doors banging, and a loud creaking sound on the landing. The eldest daughter, Tara, was fourteen years old at the time and looked nervous and highly strung. I felt immediately that I was dealing with a poltergeist. Tara said she often sensed someone standing behind her, particularly if she was on her own in the room. Things were always disappearing from her room, small items of make-up, pieces of jewellery, sometimes even items of clothing or shoes. Some of these never turned up, and occasionally her younger brother and sister might have been involved. On its own, I would not have taken this too seriously – the same thing seems to happen daily in my house, although we have no poltergeists! Combined with the other incidents reported, however, it seemed to point to polterkinetic activity centering around Tara. I worked on the house and no further incidents have been reported, but Donal tells me he 'misses it around the place'!

Another case I worked on involved very psychic twin sisters of a friend of mine. Their home is in Co. Antrim near Belfast, a modern detached house with a beautiful garden. For three years the family had been plagued by the sound of heavy footsteps tramping up the stairs at night. It sounded like two or three people and always started at 1.40 a.m. They sometimes had one or two peaceful nights, but then it would start again. Now and then, in the daytime, they heard a hammering sound in the back bedroom and occasionally footsteps in the kitchen. Twice the sound of a cough was heard directly behind one of the twins, and the other had her hair pulled just before their parents contacted me. I cleared the house for them, and though I see them regularly there have been no other incidents.

It is obvious from these accounts that Ireland as a country has more than its share of ghost stories, probably due in part to the developed psychic energies of its people. As a child, I spent a lot of time in Northern Ireland, a part of the country rich in tales of ghosts and haunted houses, such as Gilhall, near Dromore in Co. Down, and Springhill, a seventeenth-century house near Moneymore in Co. Derry, both well-documented by Sheila St Clair in *The Step on the Stair*. I have also been involved in a lot of cases in Co. Wicklow and have received reports of many more (see Chapter 11). It appears to be one of the most haunted counties in Ireland! But one thing is sure – these things exist. Rather than simply investigating them, we should be working on ways of dealing with them.

**CHAPTER 6**

# Solving the 'Halloween Case'

I FIRST HEARD OF THIS CASE several years ago, at the busiest time of my working year. Every Halloween I am in great demand for interviews and broadcasts, and these usually bring in a flood of interesting calls. A number of years ago, one particular call caught my attention. It came from a young woman who had fled her home with her two children because of spirit disturbances, and was afraid to go back. Although the family lived several hours' drive from my home, I made arrangements to visit them as soon as possible.

My friend, Ronan McKenna, agreed to accompany me and do the driving, and we set off one wet and windy evening to see for ourselves what was going on. The woman involved, who I shall call Mary, lived in the house with her one-year-old boy, Seán, and her seven-year-old daughter, Siobhán. They had been experiencing strange things in their house for about six months, and several masses had been said to no effect. Finally, the local priest advised them to leave the house and they went to stay with Mary's parents.

Most of the more unusual elements of the case centered around the baby, Seán. I treat all cases involving children as a priority, as an impressionable young mind can easily become traumatised in these situations, perhaps more because of the reactions of adults to the phenomena than because of the spirits themselves.

This was the tenth case of this nature I had dealt with and I follow approximately the same format every time. My first task is to ascertain that the disturbances are a genuine case of ghost or spirit activity and this I do by interviewing the people concerned as well as examining the house.

It transpired that this house was built near the site of a fairy fort and that the builders had been warned by local people not to build on the spot. Irish folklore maintains that to interfere in any way with a fairy fort brings bad luck. Down through the years, there are reports all over Ireland of mishaps on building sites resulting in injury and occasionally even death, supposedly as a result of invoking the wrath of the fairy folk.

Mary looked pale and tired and a little apprehensive as she began to tell me her story. It seems she first noticed crying at the back door and tapping on her kitchen window about six months after they moved in to the new house.

At first she thought it was children playing tricks, but when the disturbances persisted, Mary began to suspect that a spirit was involved. She described the noises as sounding like an animal scratching or clawing at the glass. As time went on it became louder and more insistent. Mary said she could see nothing from the window, even as the scratching was going on. Then the doorbell started ringing and from May until August the family had to live with nightly occurrences of these sounds.

Around August, the crying intensified into unearthly moaning sounds, heard by numerous friends and relatives. One such person, a close teenage relative of the family, ran out of the house in fright, and had not set foot in it since.

Many electrical disturbances began to occur around this time, the lights going on and off and the channels being changed on the television. Once, when the channel was switched while Mary was watching a programme, she told 'it' to change it back to the correct channel and to her amazement it did.

Mary thought that the spirit of someone she had forgotten to pray for was haunting her and her solution was to pray for it to stop. She began lighting candles in the church for the repose of the souls of her dead relatives. Mary is a very psychic person herself. While talking to her, I discovered that she had had a 'near death experience' (NDE) on the birth of her daughter, Siobhán.

'I had toxaemia and they took me into hospital. My blood pressure was very high and I was really ill. I was asleep and suddenly I was going down a long, dark tunnel at the end of which was a bright light. As I came nearer I saw a big gate. Jesus and the angels were there, waving their hands, telling me to go back. I didn't want to go back but they said I had to. When I woke up, the priest was there beside me and they said I nearly died.'

Her account is identical to near death experiences described in books on the subject and in parapsychological reports all over the world. In my own research, I have encountered many cases here in Ireland. All reports describe the long, dark tunnel and dazzling white light. What is seen at the end appears to be subjective images: in some cases loved ones, friends or relatives who have passed on, and are waiting. Others report seeing grassy meadows with beautiful flowers. In one report I personally received, the man involved saw a circle of native American Indians waiting to greet him. My own theory is that the subject sees an image that is particularly comforting, which in Mary's case was Jesus and the angels.

An after-effect of this type of experience appears to be a heightened psychic awareness in the subject. All of the cases I have encountered have noticed this and the majority of published cases make reference to similar discoveries. The NDE can cause an energy transformation in the individual, enhancing their extra-sensory abilities. It is not unusual to find strong intuitive talents emerging, as well as clairvoyant dreams, while healing ability frequently becomes stronger and more obvious.

I spent several hours with Mary on that first meeting, while she told me of the strange occurrences in her home. We were in the living-room of her parents' house in front of a roaring fire and it seemed incredible to hear such an odd tale in such cosy surroundings. She talked of footsteps in the night, dark shadows glimpsed around corners, objects flying across the room. She described the phenomena she had encountered in a very down-to-earth fashion, seeming almost unaware of the strangeness of her tale.

Mary had not been particularly frightened by the occurrences until the night when she went into her son's bedroom to check on him and found him jumping up and down in his cot in a sitting position, as though being bounced up and down by invisible hands. He was laughing happily and his toys floated in the air around his head. She grabbed Seán out of the cot and ran out of the room with him but there was 'not a bother on him'.

She herself turned to prayer, as she always did in an emergency. She calmed down as the child continued to play contentedly beside her on the couch. She reasoned that the child was not frightened or upset, so nothing bad or harmful could be involved. Seán had been happy and laughing, so she assumed that the spirit of a loving relative who had passed on must be involved. The rest of the night was uneventful and the family slept undisturbed. It was the night of 29 October, two days before Halloween.

The following day was peaceful in the little house, as Mary helped Siobhán to make a Halloween costume. The little girl slept in the same bedroom as her mother and that night Seán would sleep with them as well, as Mary had moved his cot into their room the night before. He was sleeping peacefully when Mary went to bed, climbing in beside her daughter as usual.

At about 4 a.m. Mary suddenly found herself wide awake and turned to look at her son in his cot. Instead of sleeping peacefully, he was gurgling happily, clutching his teddy-bear and floating about six feet in the air above his cot. She was out of bed in a flash and watched as he floated back down into his cot. She grabbed him and got back into her bed, hiding him and the still-sleeping Siobhán under the bedcovers. They soon fell asleep like this and slept undisturbed till morning.

The next day, Halloween, the house had a strange, uneasy atmosphere, remarked on by visitors. The left-hand side of the house was even more intensely cold than usual, a common feature in spirit-inhabited houses. The bedrooms lay on this side and all the people I had interviewed commented on how much colder it always was than the other side. At this stage, Mary was familiar with the signs of 'gathering energy', electrical appliances went on and off, bumping sounds were heard and the TV channels and lights went berserk. She told me she often had physical signals too, that 'things were going to happen'. Her spine would tingle, her eyes would start to water and she would feel like crying before any of the stronger manifestations. She experienced these feelings from time to time that day as she opened the door to the children collecting for the Halloween party. Most were dressed as witches and ghosts, chanting the traditional 'Any apples and nuts?' and 'Help the Halloween party'.

Mary went to sleep exhausted that night, creeping in beside her daughter while her son slumbered deeply. She woke with a start at about 1 a.m. to find Seán and his toys in mid-air again and immediately reached for the child to take him into her bed. As she took him in her arms, she felt him being pulled away from her. She saw his legs begin to rise up into the air and she began to pull him back into her arms. She was engaged in a tug-of-war with a spirit, fighting for her son. Invisible hands were pulling him up into the air by the legs. She shouted at 'it' to let go of her son and heard an answering noise fill the room. She described it as being like three or four voices, deafeningly loud, 'going right through my head'. It was like a cross between a roar and a moaning sound and as Mary pulled frantically at her son she saw a huge pair of blazing eyes, 'shining like lightbulbs', staring into hers.

'It was huge when it was close to me, like, but as it went away it got smaller and smaller. It had eyes, luminous eyes, very bright. It would blind you actually. It was like a man's face to me when it was close, but as it went away it went smaller and was like a little girl,' said Mary. With a last superhuman effort, she dragged her son firmly into her arms and went back to bed.

'I thought it was one of my own that came back to play with him. I was comfortable. I just went back to sleep and took no notice of it until the next day when I told the priest. He said I should move out. That's all he said. He said: "Get out for sure this time." So I moved out.'

Occasionally I have been called out to 'haunted houses' only to find evidence of an over-active imagination or a down-to-earth cause for the disturbances, such as noisy central heating. Each case I take on, I check very carefully for authenticity, using a variety of techniques, both psychic and scientific. In this case, I was convinced of the truth of Mary's story so the next logical step was for me to see the house.

Mary herself was unwilling to go to the house until I had worked in it, so I went there accompanied by Ronan. It was around midnight as we drove through the backroads from Mary's father's house to her little bungalow. It is a small, well-kept house, not even remotely resembling the stereotypical haunted house. There was no flash of lightning or creaking groan as the door was opened but I was amused to see that Ronan stood back to let me enter first, out of what I suspect was fear rather than politeness.

The first thing I noticed was the intense cold on the left-hand side of the house. As I was thinking this Ronan commented simultaneously on the temperature. Entering the living-room, we lit a heater and in a moment we were huddled around it warming our hands, still able to see our breath in the air. The room itself was neat and attractive, tastefully decorated with an obviously artistic eye. A door led into the kitchen at the back of the house and there I saw the windows where Mary had first experienced the scratching, clawing sounds she described. All seemed calm, almost too still and quiet, and nothing out of place occurred as we returned to the living-room.

The bedrooms were where most of the incidents took place, so we went into the first bedroom, normally occupied by Mary and her daughter. The cold seemed even more intense in the bedrooms and I remembered Mary's comment that the bedrooms were impossible to heat. The young mother's bedroom was simply furnished, the little cot pulled close to the bed as it had been on the last night they had spent there, the week before. We walked over to the cot and Ronan asked for a loan of my pendulum, which he proceeded to use in and around the cot. (The pendulum is used for dowsing or divining. It hangs from a string or thread and swings in a specific pattern in answer to questions posed by the user. Pendulums made from wood, metal or crystal can be bought in specialist shops, but a wedding ring or symmetrical bead on a piece of thread will work just as well. I 'tune in' a pendulum by saying 'My name is Sandra' and the pattern it swings indicates 'yes'. I then say 'My name is Tanith' and it swings in a different pattern, indicating a 'no'. Questions must be phrased to give a definite 'yes' or 'no' answer, and the pattern of the swing must be watched carefully, as there can be many subtle variations to lead you astray. The pendulum is a tool to enable you to communicate with your subconscious, your intuitive self. You can ask questions, pick lottery numbers, diagnose disease and locate water or metals using this simple device. Divining rods used by water diviners are a more sophisticated version of the pendulum. I occasionally use my pendulum to confirm a spirit presence in a house.)

We stood together around the cot, watching the pendulum. Suddenly I sensed a spirit presence. It was by my left shoulder and appeared to be peeping into the cot. At first I thought it was trying to see what we were doing but it left as suddenly as it appeared, seeming to shoot up into the front left-hand corner of the ceiling. I got a distinct feeling of sadness, of disappointment in fact, from the presence and I felt that the spirit had been looking for little Seán, its playmate. It was all over in a few seconds and Ronan did not appear to have noticed anything.

I felt happier and more confident after this encounter as I got a sense of the personality of the spirit and it was neither frightening nor particularly negative. We moved on then to the back bedroom, which little Seán had normally had to himself until his mother moved him into her room. Again it seemed unnaturally icy in this room but nothing occurred in there. We went out into the back garden, which was just as eerie as any other garden in the small hours of the morning, but no ghosties or ghoulies obliged by appearing.

We spent another hour in the house, huddled around the gas fire to see if we could experience any of the phenomena. By this stage I was more concerned about the temperature than the possibility of meeting a spirit! We left as dawn was beginning to streak the sky and I must admit I slept deeply during almost the entire journey back to Dublin.

November in Ireland is always a cold, wet, miserable month and, sure enough, the weather on my return journey to Mary's house was no exception. I drove through torrential rain from Dublin to help Mary as I had promised. I had a full car. There was great media interest in the case and I had been approached by many reporters and journalists who wanted to accompany me. I had no intention of turning my visit into a media circus, my main concern being for the family, so I chose my companions with care.

One of the calls was from Bernard Evans who works with RTE, the national broadcasting service. Although I had never met him, I was impressed by the work he had done in the past and felt he would adopt an intelligent and impartial stance in dealing with the story. He had also asked whether he could record the trip with a view to making a documentary and I felt this would make an interesting record of our experiences.

My first choice was Bernard and my second a freelance journalist, who turned out to be very psychic herself. We were also accompanied by my friend, Patricia, who lives within driving distance of Mary's house. I was to use her house as my base while in the area.

The next morning we set off on our journey in high spirits, as Bernard quipped, and went to collect Mary from her parents' home. We had attracted quite an entourage by the time we arrived at the house, with assorted friends and relatives of Mary's coming along to see the 'ghost buster' at work.

My first task, as I saw it in this case, was to re-balance the energies of the land the house stood on. Accompanied by Bernard, I first visited the fairy fort the local people had told us about. The day was dreadfully wet and mucky and we scrambled through briars and over fences to get to the place that I felt needed healing. I worked there for about fifteen minutes and to our delight the clouds immediately began to lift. The watery November sun emerged from behind the clouds and shone brightly, warming our backs as we headed back to the house. The group waiting in the house raised a cheer when we returned; they all felt that the appearance of the sun was a sign that I had truly healed the land.

Accompanied by Mary and Bernard, I then began my work on the house. I went from room to room, sending out thoughts of love and healing to any spirit inhabitants as I went. I first re-balanced the energies of each room, using salt, incense and gemstones. I then worked directly with the spirit energy of the place, which seemed to me to be weak everywhere except in the bedrooms.

I worked first in the back bedroom, Seán's room. I felt strongly the presence of a young girl. She seemed to be about twelve or thirteen years old but I felt that she was mentally a little slow or backward for her age. It took a while to establish direct-link communication with her as she seemed to have difficulty concentrating on anything for more than a few seconds (a feature of her personality that would have been the same before she died). I tried to question her to find out why she was so attracted to this particular place and the answer I got was 'my little brother'. That was all I could establish and while I was explaining to her that I could help her to move to a happier place, I realised she was gone.

Direct-link spirit communication is a difficult thing to achieve at the best of times, as it requires such an intense focusing of concentrated energy. It feels like sending out a probe from the third eye in the centre of the forehead, above the eyebrows, to 'attach itself' to the spirit in question. When a full link is achieved – though this is not always possible – it is similar to mental telepathy and mind-to-mind communication can then take place.

Many spirits are nervous of, or resistant to, such forms of contact and occasionally only partial-link communication or none at all can be established. In this case so far I had achieved only a partial link but was confident that I could re-establish contact and work with some success even if I could not link up properly.

Next I moved into Mary's bedroom which contained the child's cot and immediately realised that 'she' was there too. I ignored her for a moment as I would a difficult child. I pulled back the curtains and pretended to tidy the room until I sensed that she had relaxed a bit, then tried to make contact again. This time I tried to show her the Otherworld where she truly belonged. I told her that she was keeping herself in a state of unhappiness by existing neither in this world nor the next and that I could help her to move into the light where she could be among her loved ones.

She then showed me herself and her baby brother in the back of a car driven by her father. The car crashed and all three were killed. At the moment of impact, her brother was thrown out of the car through the window. Her dying thought was to find her little brother whom she adored. I told her he was in the Afterworld or Otherworld, waiting for her, along with her father. She was still a little resistant to the idea of moving on, so I just kept sending wave after wave of healing and positive energy at her to help her make up her mind. I could sense her relaxing, accepting what I was saying, and when I felt the time was right I gave her a gentle little astral 'nudge' over into the spirit world. This is hard to describe, but feels literally as though I am pushing with my mind, filled with golden light, against the spirit presence.

Helping a spirit pass over is always an incredibly tiring exercise. I immediately felt spent, physically and emotionally, usually a sign that the 'clearing' has been successful. When I rejoined the others the talk was all about how the atmosphere of the house had changed. Everyone had noticed that the temperature of the house had risen by several degrees and it was particularly obvious in the left-hand side of the house which had been so cold before. Mary herself felt happy that the spirit had gone and said she could 'feel' the difference.

We all gathered together then to form a healing circle

around Mary and her children. It was a very powerful circle, as our energies were running high and we were almost giddy from the changed atmosphere of the house. We first sent healing to the spirit of the girl and then worked directly on the mother and her children. Afterwards we had cups of tea and coffee and sandwiches and cakes and the little house was buzzing with laughter and life.

My companions and I headed back to Dublin shortly afterwards. Mary moved back into her house the next day and I was thrilled to hear that she was 'settled in with no problems', as a neighbour informed me. The aftermath for myself in Dublin involved an increase in media attention, all amazingly sympathetic – and several more calls for help from the owners of spirit-inhabited houses.

**CHAPTER 7**

# How to Tune in to Your Inner Energies

IN THE 1970s, the Irish attitude to Tarot cards, healing and spirit-healing was that they had to be evil or even 'Satanic'. In the 1980s, the prevailing attitude was that anyone, like myself, with an interest or involvement in these fields was merely 'odd' or 'weird'. Since the earth moved into the Age of Aquarius in 1987, the level of cosmic awareness in humanity in general has increased and I am happy to report that a far healthier attitude prevails today.

Evidence of this was the public reaction to the programme made by Seán Rafferty and produced by Elizabeth Kelly of BBC Ulster for 'Rafferty', called 'Spooks and Soaps', which dealt with some of the cases I had investigated. I am still working my way through the cases I encountered as a result.

It is a matter of satisfaction to me that the attitude to these matters of the spirit is changing. I am also immensely encouraged by the fact that more and more people are beginning to realise that psychic talents are a completely normal aspect of human awareness, in the same way that we can be talented in music or art. For example, anyone in the world is capable of learning to play a tune on a piano. Some will produce a painful, though recognisable sound; others will make a good attempt and the few with a marked potential will play very well, very quickly. The more practice, the better the results, no matter what level of potential one has. In the same way, anyone in the world can develop and use his or her intuitive senses to a noticeable and beneficial degree.

Most of us will have experienced 'psychic flashes' from time to time in our lives. Sometimes it consists of a premonition of personal disaster such as friends or relatives dying. There are many documented accounts of public disasters, such as aeroplanes crashing and ships sinking, which are reported *before* they happened by members of the public and not professional clairvoyants. Most of these are dismissed as coincidence or imagination by the sceptics.

Many countries in the world, however, have government-sponsored research programmes investigating the psychic sciences. Both the US and the CIS (Russia and her allies) have been active in this field since the 1920s and spend more on psychic research annually than they do on space research. The vast majority of subjects taking part in these experiments are not professional psychics but lay people chosen randomly. Huge sums of money are being spent world-wide in a long-term effort to develop more proficient and potentially useful psychic talents.

'Parapsychology' is defined in Chambers Dictionary as: 'Psychical research: the study of phenomena such as telepathy and clairvoyance which seem to suggest that the mind can gain knowledge by means other than the normal perceptual processes.'

Early researchers sought a 'sixth sense' to explain these abilities, but it has now become generally accepted that such a sixth sense does not exist. Rather, the five ordinary senses can sometimes be extended beyond their normal limitations.

Thus we have intuition (feeling), clairvoyance (seeing), clairaudience (hearing) and psychometry (touching). These are the most usually employed of the psychic senses, but many people active in this field have also experienced a paranormal sense of smell and even taste. There are numerous reports of individuals walking into an empty room and smelling the perfume used by a loved one who is now in the spirit world. This is simply a message from the loved one, a gentle reminder that he or she is still with us.

There are many other examples of these psychic powers at work on an everyday level. For instance, have you ever visited a strange house and taken an immediate dislike to one of the rooms? Have you ever decided to ring a friend for a chat only to hear the 'phone ringing and your friend on the other end of the line? Have you ever met someone who, on the surface, seemed fine but some *gut feeling* told you he or she was untrustworthy – and you were subsequently proved right?

These are all instances of psychic abilities at work. In the first example, the ability to 'sense an atmosphere' in a place or to sense a presence when there is no-one there may point to *mediumistic* talents – the ability to tune in to vibrations from the spirit world. Some people possess these talents to a marked degree without being aware of it. By that I mean that they are in tune with energies from the spirit world and receive information they often cannot interpret.

The field of professional mediumship is quite different, in that its practitioners try consciously to make contact with spirits in order to get information from them. My own attitude is to leave those in the spirit world in peace by not making any demands on them, to receive and utilise any information they send spontaneously and to give them healing when appropriate.

My second example, in which friends ring each other at the same moment, points to *telepathy*, which is simply mind-to-mind communication with another. It often occurs when people are in a highly emotional state and certain conditions seem to make it flow more easily. Many a mother suddenly has an urge to look for her child playing outside, only to find the child running towards her crying over a cut knee or similar mishap. Couples in love frequently sense things about one another and one may pick up the 'phone only to find the other trying to get through at the same time. Among friends and relatives, too, this is a frequent occurrence.

The third example relates to straightforward *intuition*, the most common of all the psychic talents. This is the inner voice we often hear advising us to avoid certain situations or actions. Properly used, it is like having a personal advisor who will help out in time of need.

Everyone is capable of experiencing a psychic occurrence. Almost every person I meet, on hearing what my profession is, has at least one such experience to relate – a dream that came true, a clairvoyant vision or a premonition. This psychic functioning appears weak and inconsistent in its natural form, occurring only occasionally and spontaneously. It requires hard work and discipline to make it flow easily and at will. It is our hidden resource, a pool of energy we can tap into to improve the quality of our lives.

I have found that those with the desire to do so can develop their psychic and healing abilities, bringing about a beneficial personal transformation. This they can do by learning to activate their own self-healing mechanism at will. The same energy is used to heal ourselves and others. Some people are interested in developing these inner resources for professional purposes but others simply wish to learn how to use them to improve the quality of their own lives and to help family and friends. To help such people, I will describe how I go about some aspects of my work and explain how anyone can follow the same methods.

In any kind of psychic work, a preliminary series of breathing exercises helps to alter one's state of consciousness and to put one in a light trance in which intuition flows more freely. 'Primary breathing', as I teach it, increases the psychic and healing energies and, even if no psychic work is involved, helps to relax one and to ease the tensions of mind, body and spirit.

First, place one hand on your chest and the other on your solar plexus, just above the waist. Breathe in slowly and deeply, counting in your mind as you inhale. If the hand on your chest raises more than the other hand, you are not breathing correctly. Try to breathe more slowly and deeply, until the hand on your chest remains still and the hand on your solar plexus rises noticeably. This tells you that you are breathing correctly and you do not need to use your hands for the rest of the exercise.

Now take note of the number you counted up to while breathing in. I take a count to five as the average number that appears comfortable for many people, but if you find four or six more comfortable stick with that. For one complete primary breath, inhale to the count of five, hold your breath for five, breathe out to the count of five and hold without breathing for five. When you try this, you may find that, when you hold your breath in or let it out, you tend to close the back of your nose. It is important that you deliberately open it again and leave it open for the energy to flow properly.

The number you count while breathing is of no importance. It is evenly paced, regular breathing that you want to achieve. As you breathe, listen to your inner voice counting and consciously will yourself to relax. Aim to banish any stray thoughts by concentrating on the counting. When you become proficient at this, you will find you can very quickly achieve a relaxed state as you begin to breathe and eventually the counting will become unnecessary.

'Solar breathing' is a useful variation on the primary breathing technique. This is an energising exercise to boost your positive, sun-energy intake and is beneficial first thing in the morning or whenever you need an energy boost. Simply place a finger over your left nostril when you begin your primary breathing, so that your first complete breath (in and out) is taken through your right nostril. Cover your right nostril and breathe through your left for your second complete breath, then change nostrils again for your third. Continue covering alternate nostrils as you breathe and finish by breathing through your right nostril on the last complete breath of the exercise.

For 'lunar breathing' you reverse the process, beginning and ending the cycle by covering the right nostril and breathing through the left. This produces a receptive, passive energy, the energy of the moon, and is very relaxing in moments of extreme stress or tension and can help induce sleep.

I combine two types of healing in my work: projective energy (touch) therapy, also known as laying on of hands, and visualisation therapy, which can be used for absent healing. The most important thing to keep in mind if you want to heal is that you are aiming to help the person you are working on to feel better. If you are hoping to perform miracles you will be disappointed in your own results and this will slow down the development of your skill. If you are relaxed and confident this will allow your healing energy to flow freely and the more you use it the more it develops.

## TOUCH THERAPY

If you want to develop healing hands, here is a simple way to start. (Children and animals make extremely good guinea pigs to practise on at first.) First, wash your hands and let the tapwater flow down your hands and fingers. Visualise it cleansing and purifying your hands for the purpose of healing. Pat them dry and then rub them together until you feel them begin to warm up (this helps to stimulate the flow of energy). Now place your hands, palms down, on top of the head of the person you are working with and concentrate on your hands as they begin to grow warm and tingling. Feel the flow from your hands to the person you are healing and learn to focus on your hands so that you are thinking and feeling with them. Breathe slowly and deeply and send thoughts of love and healing to the person you are working on.

Now take your right hand and place the centre of the palm on the person's forehead, with your left hand in the same position on the back of the person's head. Feel the energy pass through the head from hand to hand, soothing and healing. The centre of the palm of each hand contains a mini-*chakra* or energy centre, and this exercise is excellent for calming mental and emotional confusion as well as physical ailments.

Next, move your hands down to the neck and, placing a hand

on each side of the neck, work there before moving down to the shoulders. Spend only a couple of minutes working at each position or you may feel drained after the session. At this point, if the person you are working on has a specific problem area, for instance, a sore knee, move on to work on that. Place your hands on either side of the knee and work there for about five minutes. Although I call this touch therapy, strictly speaking it is not necessary to touch the person you are working on. Holding your hands, as described above, at a distance of one to two inches away from the body is equally effective.

## VISUALISATION THERAPY

The person you wish to heal does not have to be in the same room as you or even in the same country. I use three different methods of utilising the visualisation faculty, which I have developed intuitively over the years. All are equally effective. If you have a photograph of the person you wish to heal, you can use the method I call photo-visualisation. Place the photograph on a smooth surface, such as a table, in front of you. Prepare your hands for healing, as outlined above, and rest them lightly, palms down, on the photo in front of you. Then close your eyes and start some slow, even breathing to bring you into a meditative state.

In your mind's eye *see* the person in the photograph in the room with you, *picture* him or her sitting in front of you. The success of this technique depends on your ability to see or picture the target, as distinct from thinking of or imagining the person. It is also important to project this image into the present or future, so try not to remember the person as you last saw them as this will not produce the correct energy for successful healing.

When you have reached a stage where you can picture the person, picture yourself with your hands on his or her head. Then let the healing energy flow as though you were performing contact healing. I usually give a little 'push' in my mind to start it flowing. You will recognise your own healing energy as a form of heat, tingling, throbbing or itching in your hands. Many experience a swollen sensation, as though the hands are getting bigger.

The second technique is useful if you do not have a photograph of the person you wish to heal. Visualise yourself standing with the person sitting in front of you. With eyes closed, hold your hands side by side as though above the person's head. Visualise their head under your hands as you send healing, and picture the person's smiling face. This is a widely used technique known as 'absent healing'.

Another visualisation method I use involves programming a crystal by charging it with your hands while repeating 'This is to heal [name]' several times. Place the crystal in front of you and, covering it with both hands, pour golden healing light through the crystal to the person you wish to heal. Visualise them smiling and looking well as you do this. Healing energy is effective not only in cases of physical ailments, but will help if the person has emotional problems, financial worries or any other problem.

There are many misconceptions about the use of psychic and healing abilities, the commonest being that they are possessed only by the chosen few who belong to some religion or cult. Many of these myths are now being dispelled by the enormous amount of information available on the subject. Yet the inclination still remains among many practitioners to claim great 'powers' which are supposedly supernatural in origin.

## How to Tune in to Your Inner Energies

The truth of the matter is that, as I have already pointed out, we can all do these things. Every one of us can accurately predict the future or make someone feel better by laying on of hands. We can vastly improve these natural abilities, as with any talent, by learning the techniques, having the belief in ourselves to exercise them with confidence and, finally, through practice. There really is no 'right way' or 'wrong way' to do these things. I teach my students my methods to use as a guideline but I encourage them to develop their own methods through trial and error. If it feels comfortable for you to do things in a particular way, then that is the method that suits you best. You will find it easy to develop your inner skills if you go with your own intuitive flow.

# CHAPTER 8

# Techniques in Spirit Work

WHEN DOING ANY KIND OF TRANCE or spirit work, I use certain techniques which are essential to the proper focusing and projection of my psychic energies. These are more difficult to learn than the breathing exercises already described in Chapter 7, as they demand a much higher degree of concentration and the exercise of mental and spiritual qualities as well as physical ones. There is also a certain element of risk in some of the work I do, for example, those of a nervous temperament could become traumatised if a spirit manifested itself to them. I advise students not to attempt any work involving spirits unless they are satisfied that they are fully conversant with the necessary techniques. These are called 'meditation', 'grounding' and 'centering'.

## MEDITATION

This technique requires a suitable place, a quiet room or, when the weather permits, a peaceful spot outdoors. Noise will disturb the meditation so it is essential to find somewhere quiet. Meditate alone – no matter how close you are to

## Techniques in Spirit Work

someone their presence will distract you. Allow at least one-and-a-half hours to elapse after a meal, have a good wash or a bath, dress comfortably and take up your meditation position. Sit on the floor, or on cushions if you wish. Do not lean your back against a wall or chair or any other support. If you are able to assume the full lotus position, sitting with the left foot crossed on to the right thigh, and the right foot crossed on to the left thigh, then do so. If you do not find this position comfortable, practise it for a few minutes every day until you do. Do not force this posture, let it come gradually and eventually you will be supple enough to sit in the lotus position for meditation. In the meantime, sitting on the floor cross-legged will do. Whatever position you adopt it must fulfill three conditions: comfort, a straight back, and easy breathing.

Having assumed your position, ignore all the distracting thoughts which are running through your mind. Do not fight these thoughts, but as they arise, look at them as though they did not belong to or concern you. If you fight them back violently, they will only intensify and take away your concentration. Instead of giving consideration to them, project a thought of well-being towards all living creatures in front of you to infinity. This thought must not be directed at any particular individual, it must be all-encompassing, as if rays of good-will were emanating to all beings ahead of you. On no account must the rays be visualised as returning to you.

When you are satisfied that the thought has projected without any feeling of self-interest, the same procedure should be enacted to the right side, without turning the head. Then, still looking ahead, the thought should be projected behind you, to the back, then to the left. Next, beneath you and lastly, above you. This can stand on its own as a good exercise, but it also works as a good introduction to meditation.

**STAGE ONE**: Sitting in your chosen position, with the right hand resting flat on the palm of the left hand, with the tips of the two thumbs touching, lightly close the eyes and, keeping your back straight, start breathing gently to a mental count of five. Breathe in slowly to 'one', breathe out to 'two', in to 'three', and so on. After the fifth breath, start again at 'one', and repeat the process. Make the count at the end of each breath as this will help you to establish a precise rhythm. Fix your attention on the breath going in and out of the nostrils, concentrating on the point just under the nose where the breath enters and leaves. The breath should not be followed internally or externally. Pay no attention to what happens 'outside', simply watch the breaths going in and out of the nostrils to the rhythm of the count. The purpose of this part of the practice is to gain concentration which will lead to a state of full meditation. How long you should continue with this stage depends on how soon you are able to concentrate on the breath alone, without counting. This will vary from person to person, according to how well-developed your powers of concentration were before practice was first begun. When, after a few days or weeks of regular practice, you can dispense with the counting, you are ready to commence the next stage.

**STAGE TWO**: By this stage you can practise the breathing without counting but your mind may have a tendency to wander. Instead of counting, you must now 'follow the breath' with your mind down through the nostrils inside and to a spot just below the rib-cage, the solar plexus, and back out again, repeating the process over and over. These are the limits and

*Techniques in Spirit Work*

they should not be exceeded. Some people feel unsure as to where exactly the solar plexus is, but there is no need for concern. If you do not follow the breaths below the point where the two lower ribs spread from the centre of the body, or even to the navel, you will not exceed the necessary area of concentration. Practise this stage until the observation of the breath becomes automatic.

**STAGE THREE**: Now you must focus on the breath entering and leaving the nostrils. This is done without counting, and without following the breath inside the body. The previous two stages have eliminated those necessities, and you should be able to concentrate on breathing rhythmically, as in the first stage, with an automatic consciousness of the swing of each breath from nostrils to solar plexus, as in the second stage. You will find, in fact, that your breathing tends to become shallow. This is because it is becoming refined. Up to now consciousness of, and concentration upon, your breathing has been the 'object' used for this meditation. Now you have trained your body and mind into a state of purity by following the practice faithfully in all of its aspects, and are sliding gently into lighter and lighter breathing of which you are still aware until at last you slip into a state where your breathing is barely perceptible.

This is the state of meditation in which powerful healing and self-healing can take place. Problem-solving becomes easy and inspiration flows freely. You can meditate with or without a specific purpose, and if you fix a goal firmly in your mind before beginning the exercise, you will be programming your subconscious for success as you meditate.

## GROUNDING

Grounding or 'earthing' means connecting with the earth's energies. The best way to do this is by sitting on the ground, preferably out of doors. Sit in a comfortable position with your eyes closed and your head and spine as straight as possible. This enables the energy to flow freely up your spine, energising your *chakras* or energy centres.

Begin to breathe slowly and deeply, using the primary breathing technique described in the previous chapter. Draw the breath in to all parts of your body, wherever you need to relax and let go, releasing all tension as you exhale. Now feel how you are sitting, where you touch the ground, how your body touches the ground. Feel the magnetic pull between the earth and your body. Picture your spine as an open channel between sky and earth. See the bright, green energy flow up from the earth through this channel and pour out through the top of your head, flowing into the cosmos.

Then, picture bright, golden light, pouring from the soles of your feet into the earth, connecting you to her solid strength. Picture a shining ray of energy flowing down your spine. This is your 'grounding cord', extending like a root into the earth from the base of your spine. Picture it flowing deep, deep down to connect with the fiery core at the earth's centre. Connect with this source and feel the earth energy rising in you like sap in a tree. Any tensions or energy imbalances you want to correct, send them down your grounding cord for transformation, as the purifying fires of the inner earth will transmute them into positive, golden energy.

This is an extremely powerful exercise and, as with most breathing techniques, it is not advisable to stand up suddenly after doing this as you may experience dizziness. I use this type of exercise to relax and to dispel any nervousness I might feel when working on a 'haunted house' or at any time when I feel I need extra strength or endurance.

## CENTERING

The technique I call 'centering' is really a way of helping the mind, body and spirit to function in harmony. This exercise is extremely beneficial, particularly when you need to focus your energies for a specific purpose or to deal with a particular task. It helps increase your powers of concentration, and re-balances the energies after times of illness or stress.

Sitting in a comfortable position, with the spine held straight, begin breathing slowly and deeply, as in the primary breathing exercise referred to in Chapter 7. Place both hands on your solar plexus, just above the waist. As you breathe, visualise bright, golden light pouring in through the top of your head and being drawn deep into your solar plexus. Bright, golden light pours in through your hands, energising your solar plexus, creating a radiating mass of energy at the centre of your being. When this area feels bright, light and golden, begin to concentrate on your feet. Feel the soles begin to tingle as bright, green earth energy is drawn up through your feet. Feel your legs glow with this green energy as it is drawn steadily up to your solar plexus. Now see the golden-green light grow strong and bright, strengthening and healing mind, body and spirit. Now place your hands on your head, and 'pull' the golden-green energy up into your head, sending it down through your arms to your hands. Feel any stress, worries or confusion being erased by this bright light, and finish by placing the palm of your right hand on your third eye in the centre of the forehead and your left hand at the centre of the back of your head. Imagine golden-green light pouring back and forth between your two hands. The whole exercise should take no more than about five minutes. Finish by pressing your palms together for a few moments as you return your breathing to normal. Rest for a few moments before standing.

The purpose of all psychic exercises is to contact, communicate with, or programme the subconscious mind in some way. When we are asleep, the conscious mind is at rest, and much of our dream content comprises material from the subconscious. This is an untapped source of psychic material which most of us unfortunately neglect.

Since the dawn of civilisation, man has been aware of the power of dreams. The ancient Egyptians, Babylonians, Assyrians and Romans, to name but a few, all studied and analysed their dreams, interpreting the symbols to predict future events. Most dreams take the form of visual images. Carl Jung, the brilliant Swiss psychiatrist and psychologist, wrote that 'visual images have the quality of the human soul', through visual images we can explore the human mind as well.

Sessions with my weekly psychic study group involve interpreting the visual images we receive in dreams on several levels – psychological, physical, spiritual. For example, a dream about a snake may refer to your sexuality, the snake being traditionally a phallic symbol, while at the same time warning you that someone around you is not to be trusted, literally, a 'snake in the grass'. The same symbol may be telling you, on a spiritual level, that you are undergoing a valuable transformation leading to the emergence of new aspects of your self, just as the snake sheds its skin. On a psychic level, the dream may actually be a prediction, warning you of an encounter with a snake – even in the zoo or on TV.

*Techniques in Spirit Work*

Such precognition is a most unusual ability in terms of our conventional notions of time and free will, and is often unrecognised by those who have this gift until they begin to notice that their dreams often do predict events. It is actually a very common experience to dream about an event before it happens, yet almost all such experiences are dismissed as mere coincidence. In the 1930s, Dame Edith Lyttleton invited listeners to the BBC to send her their reports on personal psychic experiences of this type. The response was overwhelming. Precognitive and clairvoyant dreams offer one of the richest sources of precognition. Dame Lyttleton wrote an account of these experiences in her book *Some Cases of Prediction*, and she presents dreams which relate to a wide range of subject matter, from personal tragedies to international disasters, but the greatest number of cases involved dreaming the results of horse races and other sporting events! Many of the dreamers had no great interest in these sports, and almost all reports were of a once-off experience. In 1950 John Godley wrote his book *Tell Me the Next One* in which he tells how he dreamt the names of seven winning horses, winning money each time he dreamt. One night he dreamt of two races and, feeling sure he had two winners, he contacted the *New York Times* office in London hoping to get some money from his story if the horses won. The *Times* suggested he contact the *Daily Mirror* who agreed to buy the story if the horses won. They did, and the *Mirror* not only published the story but offered him a job. Godley dreamt the names of horses or very close approximations, but more common nowadays is the dreaming of numbers for the Lottery. I have two clients who have won huge sums in Ireland's Lotto and both are convinced that their dreams helped them win.

We all dream every night though many people remember nothing in the morning. One enjoyable part of my work is helping people to remember their dreams. I often have to overcome scepticism, of course. In my very first group, one member firmly declared that he never had dreams and seemed not to believe me when I told him that everyone does. I suggested he take a notebook and pencil to bed with him and mentally programme himself to remember his dreams when he woke up by using an affirmation. I recommended he repeat over and over in his mind before going to sleep, 'I will recall my dreams clearly in the morning.' I also showed him how to programme a piece of quartz crystal for the same purpose. The crystal is cleansed, then charged by transmitting energy from the hands into the stone (see Chapter 3). The stone is programmed by repeating in your mind the phrase 'To help me to recall my dreams' as you charge it.

Finally, I explained that, in order to retrieve as much dream material as possible, he should come to consciousness slowly in the morning instead of leaping straight out of bed. He was impressed when, the second morning that he followed my instructions, he remembered snatches of his dreams. Within two weeks, the entries in his notebook were averaging two pages daily. Not bad for someone who 'never had dreams'!

Some dreams are predictive, that is, they foretell or warn against some future event. Often, these may be small, everyday incidents. For example, in the case of Ann-Marie, described in Chapter 4, the night before she first came to see me she dreamt of two black cats. When she arrived at my house, she was met on the doorstep by my two black cats, Nomi and Fellini. I call this sort of experience 'trivia clairvoyance', because it is simply a symptom that the dreamer has clairvoyant ability.

Vague, half-remembered dreams are unlikely to have any important significance. Other dreams not worth interpreting include those which occur after over-eating or over-indulgence in alcohol or drugs. Dreams of falling, flying or floating in space are all symptoms of astral projection. These dreams, as well as those about being fully or partially undressed or being unable to move or cry for help in a situation of danger, are common and have no psychic significance. Dreams which occur during illness, shock or any negative conditions in your life will seldom be predictive, nor will those concerning people, situations or things connected to your life during the preceding day.

Many common dreams are known as 'dreams of contrary', that is, they predict the opposite of what occurs in the dream. To dream of a death can often predict a birth, while a funeral may indicate an engagement, wedding or other form of celebration. To dream of being very wealthy – if you are not – may foretell a time of financial hardship. To dream of being lonely or alone predicts a new friendship or relationship, while to dream of fighting predicts a time of harmony with friends and family. Many of the more frightening or negative dream symbols signify the reverse. Other dreams are straightforward in their interpretation. To dream you are smiling or to see others smiling means you will soon have very good luck. To dream of your relatives indicates an increase in financial or emotional security, while to dream of going on holiday signifies an increase in finance. These examples point to the trends you can expect in your life after such a dream, but for a more in-depth interpretation, examination of every detail of the dream is necessary.

Dreams may also be warning you about something you are picking up on a subconscious level during your waking hours.

A client of mine phoned to tell me that three times in one week she dreamt that a wheel fell off her car as she was driving. She asked me what the dream meant, and my reply was 'Have you checked the nuts on the wheels?' She hadn't, and went away to do so. She then told me that the nuts on one wheel were so loose that the wheel was about to come off. My client interpreted this as a psychic experience. I feel that on a subconscious level she had noticed some difference in the sound of the wheel as she drove, and she received this information in her dream. When you wish to interpret a dream, first look for the most obvious message it conveys, as this is often the answer.

Messages from the spirit world often come in the form of dreams. Many people receive messages from their loved ones in the Afterworld while they are sleeping and generally they report a feeling of well-being after such a dream. This is a favourite way of communication by those who have passed on and it is far less frightening to dream of a loved one looking well and happy than to wake up one night to see an apparition at the foot of the bed.

Predictive dreams usually occur when we are sleeping most deeply, generally between 2 a.m. and 7 a.m. A dream that is clear and vivid is an indication of the importance of the event or warning forecast. Such dreams, especially if they feature bright colours, are well worth interpreting, as colours can point to extra-sensory perception (ESP) at work.

To interpret your dreams accurately requires some effort and practice but it is by no means difficult. I advised my group members to invest in a good book of dream symbols and to write down what they remembered immediately on waking. Dreams are made up of many elements and it is important to analyse even the smallest detail. Emotions you felt in the dream, such as sorrow, joy, anger or fear, must be taken carefully into account. As a general guideline, upward movement (climbing stairs, walking uphill, etc.) signify advancement or success while downward movement forecasts problems or setbacks. Clean or shiny objects or conditions are omens of success; dirty or dull ones predict difficulties.

Dreams featuring a mixture of bright colours, with no one colour predominating, forecast increasing security, success and advancement. Each colour can tell you something different. Here is the list I compiled through working with the group.

### DREAM COLOUR SIGNIFICANCE

*Black:* Indicates reverses or problems and warns that this is not a time for taking risks, for gambling or for speculation of any kind.

*Blue:* Forecasts help coming from an unexpected source and/or the solution of a problem.

*Brown:* Financial success, possibly a windfall.

*Green:* Predicts travel and/or news from abroad.

*Grey:* Indicates a period of waiting for something, marking time, a passive phase. Sometimes predicts a legal situation in the offing.

*Lavender, Lilac, Mauve:* The paler shades of violet foretell minor disappointments, delays or petty irritations.

*Orange:* Advises you to be patient and to expect delays concerning an anticipated change in your circumstances.

*Pink:* An excellent omen of success, which also predicts happiness in an established relationship or a new romance on the way.

*Purple:* Refers to legal matters or signing of legal papers and indicates success in business affairs.

*Red, bright:* A sign of passion and energy. Can indicate unexpected romantic developments ... but beware of losing your temper!

*Red, dark:* Wine, plum or maroon all forecast an increase in social activity, unexpected good news and invitations.

*White:* Indicates success in all your current undertakings and good luck in business or finance.

*Yellow:* Look out for some creative inspiration. Also predicts a period of minor setbacks before successful achievement of a goal.

**CHAPTER 9**

# The Powers of Stones and Crystals

DOWN THROUGH THE AGES, since the beginning of time, the beauty of gems and precious stones has held a fascination for mankind. Ancient wisdom claimed that these stones had marvellous powers, which varied according to the inherent energies of each type of gem. Originally, they were used by prehistoric man as amulets or talismans to ward off evil or to bestow their positive attributes on the wearer.

Later generations revered the stones as deities and used them in a variety of religious, ritualistic and magical ways. They were offered as sacrifices and often buried in the earth as part of ancient fertility rites. Their primary use in more recent years has been for decorative purposes and they are widely used in jewellery. Recently, however, there has been a revival of interest in the hidden properties of the stones. Many of them possess healing energies and are the basis for New Age crystal and gemstone therapies. Modern science has also found many uses for crystals, such as in watches and in the field of telecommunications.

Since childhood I have been fascinated by precious and semi-precious gemstones. My parents were a flamboyant couple and our house was full of beautiful and interesting stones, many bought while they were on their travels around the world, others found on the beach here and abroad. From my mother I inherited a love of unusual jewellery. To this day, she has the most amazing collection of unusual pieces and is famous for her large rings.

I remember as a child being lost, entranced, in the golden glow of an enormous topaz my mother wore on her right hand. I would stare into the stone and get delicious glimpses of strange and wonderful things, hints of a magical world deep inside the fire of the stone. I was always drawn to stones and could never walk past a jeweller's shop-window without immersing myself in the beauty of diamonds, emeralds and sapphires, which seemed to flash and gleam in my direction.

In 1970, my mother and I joined the Lapidary Society in Dublin to learn more about the stones. Having become able to identify many of the different types of precious and semi-precious gems, I then began my own research into their hidden properties. I had noticed that wearing certain stones had an effect, subtle but noticeable, on my moods and even sometimes on my physical condition. For example, I once put on an amethyst pendant while suffering from a sinus infection and noticed that it seemed to have a clearing effect on my blocked nose. I began to try it out any time I encountered friends or clients with sinus problems and I got excellent feedback regarding its efficacy.

It can take several months to tune into the full range of energies possessed by each stone but this type of personal research always proves immensely rewarding in more ways than one might expect. Wearing or carrying stones actually 'spring-cleans' your aura and you tend to feel energised in some way as a result.

The stones can influence mind, body and spirit by diffusing their subtle energies into the aura. Their beauty has an effect on the most insensitive and sceptical of people and even hardened disbelievers can be found wearing an item of jewellery containing their birthstone for good luck.

Superstitions abound about different stones. Emeralds and pearls are both considered unlucky for brides in Ireland; in India, however, the bride wears pearls to ensure good luck and happiness in her marriage. Jet, a black stone popular in Victorian times, is traditionally associated with mourning. It was used for magical and ceremonial purposes by the druids, and knives made of jet have been found at Stonehenge in England. In olden times in Ireland, sailors' wives would burn a piece of jet to ensure their husbands' safe return from stormy seas. According to tradition, wearing an amethyst is said to prevent drunkenness – but I'm afraid my own research into this shows it to be definitely untrue!

Many stones, particularly crystals, often seem to 'disappear' from where you have put them. They will reappear, believe it or not, when you have need of them again, so don't be alarmed when this happens. It is almost as if they decide when you do and don't need their energies. Certain stones can change colour according to the mood or physical well-being of the wearer and this has specific significance. Turquoise, for example, is often given as a token of love; if the wearer's love fades, however, the stone will fade in colour too.

Coral is, properly speaking, not a gemstone, although it can be used for the same purposes. Formed on the seabed, it is composed of the skeletons of tiny marine animals. It varies in colour from white to pale pink to deep reddish-pink, and is commonly used in jewellery. It symbolises life-force energy, and was widely used as a protection against the evil eye. It is also said to grow pale in colour if the wearer becomes ill. It was considered a sacred stone among the native American Indian and Tibetan peoples.

Quartz crystals used to be found frequently on Irish beaches but, since the revival of crystal consciousness, they are few and far between. My daughter Tanith and I came across some last year in Ballycanew in Co. Wexford and we gathered fifteen small-to-medium sized crystals in an afternoon, our personal record so far. I also found three beautiful crystals on the beach in Dingle, Co. Kerry, two years ago.

My children and I have special places we go to collect pyrites, known as 'fool's gold'. If we wish to travel farther afield to collect stones, there is a disused amethyst mine on Achill Island in Co. Mayo.

My home is full of crystals and stones of different types. Many I have found myself but most I have bought or received as presents. Clients of mine have brought me stones for my collection from literally the four corners of the globe. When I first visit a spirit-inhabited house, I bring some crystals and different forms of quartz with me to leave there until my next visit. I charge them beforehand to purify and re-balance the energies of the land and building. This, in a way, prepares the house, 'primes' it, so to speak, for the healing work I intend to do there.

The stones I find most effective in spirit healing and energy re-balancing are snow quartz, rose quartz, very pale pieces of amethyst, rock crystal and clear calcite, either in combination or separately. I leave a piece at every entrance and exit to the house, over the centre of each door and on each windowsill to form a protective barrier around the house. I also leave some in the fireplaces, hot-press, etc., and ask that they are left undisturbed until I return. I can then use these stones as conductors for absent healing. I send positive healing to the house and its inhabitants until my next visit. In one house, a very large chunk of rose quartz disappeared between my first and second visit and, to my knowledge, has never surfaced since. Stolen by a lovesick ghost, perhaps?

When I go to perform the actual 'clearing' on a house the first thing I do is to cleanse and purify these stones carefully, as I described in Chapter 3. When the clearing and healing are finished, I recharge the same stones and leave them in place for another couple of weeks. This generally has quite a comforting effect on the inhabitants who, of course, have only my word that I can remove the spirit presence from their home.

I once got a panicky phone call from a very psychic old lady whose house I had cleared. She had seen a workman move one of the stones when preparing to paint her woodwork and she was worried that her former house-spirit might return. She had experienced doors slamming, footsteps going up and down stairs and thumping sounds in her attic at night for about thirty years. After I worked in her house, she told me she was sleeping soundly at night for the first time in years. I reassured her that no harm would come from moving the stones. When the time came to remove them I did offer to give her a present of them. She was delighted because they gave her a sense of security and they still remain in the same places to this day, nearly ten years since the clearing.

As a self-styled purveyor of the weird and wonderful, I advise you to explore the fantastic world of stones and crystals and see for yourself what powers they really have.

When you buy a gemstone or crystal, you must cleanse it before using it by washing it in sea-water, or salt and water, and rinsing it well in cold, running water. This clears any negative energies from the stone and releases its natural powers. If you want to wear your stone as jewellery, you will experience the best results if the stone makes contact with your skin. If using an un-set stone, carry it in your left-hand side pocket to receive its energies. Usually, your *left* hand draws energy to you and your *right* hand sends out energy. (The reverse may sometimes prove true for those who are left-handed, so try both ways and see which works best for you.)

You can transmit your stone's healing powers to someone else by simply holding the gem in your right hand and visualising the person you want to send healing to. It is important to picture the person in good health and happy, as you do it. This is one of the basic methods of absent crystal healing.

Many stones have similar properties and you may find it difficult to decide which suits you best. If you find a stone particularly beautiful to look at or you find yourself drawn to touch one particular stone, then that is the stone for you. Gemstones often choose you rather than *vice-versa* by 'winking' at you to catch your eye. Quite often you may go home after looking at stones and find that one particular stone keeps coming into your mind, either because of its appearance or its name. Again, this is the stone for you.

Stones add a noticeable energy to the room in which they are kept. Large quartz crystals kept in a room will actually energise the whole house. They send out soothing, healing vibrations of positive energy which are immediately noticeable, even to the most sceptical. Certain combinations of stone can be even more effective than single stones, because the energies blend in such a way as to produce a new and even more effective form of energy. Snow quartz and clear calcite, for example, enhance and amplify the qualities of almost every other stone.

Crystals and gemstones can be very effective tools in all forms of healing and self-healing. For simple self-healing, first select the stone you feel most suitable for your needs. If in doubt, quartz crystal is a good stone to use. Simply hold the stone in the centre of the palm of your left hand, covering it loosely with the right hand. Picture a beam of pure white light travelling through the stone and into your left hand. Imagine this light travelling up your arm, then down your chest to light up your heart. Feel your heart throbbing with bright, white light, then watch the light travel down into your solar plexus. Now feel bright, white light pouring in through the top of your head, then down your body to your feet. Finish by holding the stone against your third eye for two or three minutes.

To send healing to others, simply hold the stone in the palm of your right hand. Picture the person you wish to heal looking well, healthy and happy. See them glow with energy transmitted through the stone (white light if using crystal, otherwise the colour of the stone). Do not use black stones for this type of exercise, they are best simply carried or worn.

The following are some of the more commonly available stones and their properties. These are my favourites and the properties attributed to them are a result of my own research:

*Agate* (many shades of brown, orange, red, green, blue, as well as multicoloured varieties): Considered a very lucky stone in all its forms, each shade of agate has different properties. All agates have properties of fruitfulness, inner strength and longevity. They are freely available and inexpensive to buy.

*Agate, banded* (commonly browns, white, black): Traditionally a very lucky stone, banded agate gives protection, restores bodily energy and eases stress. It increases self-confidence and helps to attract love and friendship. Brings success in all your undertakings and helps to prevent illness and to prolong life.

*Agate, black*: Gives courage, aids in competitions and examinations and is an excellent stone for grounding and centering (for techniques, see Chapter 8). Very important in all types of psychic and spirit work.

*Agate, black and white*: Guards against physical danger and helps develop intuition and give direction in life by uncovering hidden potential. Helps promote abundance, so it is particularly good for writers, musicians and anyone wanting to increase his or her creative potential. It calms and refreshes the mind, body and spirit, so is excellent for preventing depression, panic attacks and other nervous conditions.

*Agate, blue lace* (variegated pale blue): The stone of peace, happiness and contentment, it aids relaxation and combats stress. It also intensifies the creative energy flow, so is excellent for artists, musicians, actors and anyone involved in writing or the media.

*Agate, brown or tawny*: The stone of success, it attracts material good fortune and financial luck. Helps the owner to achieve progress in all undertakings, so it is a powerful aid during exams, interviews, etc. It is a very good all-healing stone and protects against infections and skin problems.

*Agate, green*: Good for strengthening the eyes and developing clairvoyance and healing abilities.

*Agate, leopardskin* (yellow/brown mottled): An invaluable aid to concentration and study and excellent for past-life work and regression.

*Agate, moss* (green): A lucky stone for gardeners who often bury them in the soil. They can also be placed among the roots of fruit trees or hung in the branches to increase the yield. It also helps overcome shyness and aids in making friends.

*Agate, red*: This stone has healing and calming properties and is good for ailments of the blood. Also excellent for overcoming shyness and increasing self-confidence.

*Agate, turitella* (multicoloured black, brown, grey, pinkish patterns): Helps access and develop inner energies and enhances all types of past-life work.

*Amazonite*: This beautiful blue/green stone is the traditional stone of gamblers, as it attracts financial luck. An extremely popular New Age stone, it also possesses strong spiritual qualities, helping to uncover hidden talents, especially psychic and creative potential. It helps to increase self-confidence, control negative emotions and has soothing, calming, and relaxing qualities.

*Amethyst* (pale lilac to deepest purple): A form of quartz and the stone of peace, amethyst is excellent for reducing stress and promoting peaceful sleep. It is a powerful aid to developing clairvoyant abilities. Helps fight off infection and is good for sinus problems, headaches and depression. Amethyst is also a powerful pain-killer, soothing emotional as well as physical pain. It calms fears, raises hopes and generally lifts the spirits. A stone of true love, it is often exchanged by lovers to strengthen their commitment. Helps overcome drug and alcohol abuse problems and traditionally believed to increase the beauty and power of attraction of the wearer. It is also a spiritual stone and is an excellent aid during meditation and all forms of psychic and healing work.

*Aquamarine* (transparent, pale blue or blueish-green): This was the stone of the sea-goddess in ancient times and is still associated with the sea and the element of water and as a result is particularly lucky for the water signs of the zodiac. Aquamarine has cleansing and purifying qualities, so is particularly effective for skin problems, infections, cancerous conditions, etc. Also very effective for throat and glandular problems and disorders of the neck, jaw and teeth. This is the stone of mystics and seers.

*Aventurine* (pale to deep green): Stimulates creativity and aids in studies. Brings financial luck, enhances business abilities and is a powerful all-round healing and lucky stone. Improves eyesight.

*Beryl* (blue and green): A stone for attracting love and harmony. Aids in developing psychic abilities and improving memory. Helps in liver problems, swollen glands and eye problems.

*Blue John* (colour varies, mainly blue, purple and yellow, sometimes veined with white, brown or black inclusions):

A form of fluorite, this beautiful stone is found only in Derbyshire. Blue John helps relieve stress and tension and has pain-killing properties, particularly for rheumatic problems. It is an excellent stone for increasing confidence and inducing creative inspiration.

*Calcite, clear* (translucent, white stone): This stone possess the unique optical quality of double refraction, that is, if you look through a piece of calcite at a line drawn on a page, the line appears to be doubled. Its main power, then, is the property of doubling the effects of other stones and amplifying their natural energies. Also clears negative vibrations from property when used with quartz crystal or rose quartz.

*Carnelian* (orange/red): Promotes peace and harmony and dispels depression. It strengthens the voice, increases self-confidence and eloquence and is good for communication and public speaking. Helps prevent skin diseases, nosebleeds and aids in sexual problems. It is the stone of friendship and faithfulness.

*Celestite* (pale blue, translucent): A magnificent stone useful for all types of psychic and inspirational work. It also removes physical and mental stress and tension.

*Citrine* (golden-yellow): A form of quartz, this is a powerful healing stone, especially effective for the kidneys and digestive system, the endocrine glands and in cases of diabetes. Excellent for relaxation and restful sleep, it gives the wearer control over the emotions. Relieves depression and stimulates psychic awareness.

*Garnet, red*: This is the stone of love and passion, romance and fidelity. Brings happiness in love and promotes sincerity and devotion. An excellent healer for heart problems and helps soothe inflammation and disorders of the blood.

*Haematite* (silver/black): An excellent aid in drawing illness from the body and strengthening the immune system. It energises and promotes alertness and is a good focus for meditation. Brings success in legal matters.

*Jasper, red:* Known as the 'Mother of Stones', it is excellent during pregnancy and childbirth and for mothers in general. Strengthens the heart when mourning the loss of a loved one. A soothing, comforting stone.

*Jasper, green* An excellent healing stone, it also helps prevent illness. Good for speeding-up convalescence and promoting restful sleep. Attracts financial good fortune.

*Kunzite* (pink, lilac and white): A stone of harmony, balance and relaxation, kunzite is excellent for all types of muscular stress and tension. Calms and soothes anger and fear.

*Lepidolite* (lilac/pink): A beautiful stone which helps control negative emotions. Placed under the pillow, it helps banish nightmares. Pieces containing pink tourmaline are particularly lucky for love and are often exchanged by lovers.

*Malachite* (green with dark green and black patterns): The sacred stone of the Egyptians, this is one of the most powerful stones of all. It helps to attract love, money and business success, increases business abilities and develops self-confidence. It expands one's ability to love and brings emotional peace. The guardian stone of travellers, it protects against accidents and misfortune. An unsurpassed healer, it heals and balances the whole system. It is particularly effective for eye infections, asthma and bronchitis, rheumatism and arthritis, gynaecological and menstrual problems.

*Moonstone* (pearly white, often blue or cream tones): Traditionally the sacred stone of the moon goddesses, this stone draws love and affection. It also helps to sort out problems between lovers and brings clarity of thought in times of confusion. It is a very powerful aid to slimming, giving up smoking or any form of addiction problem. This is also the stone prized by psychics as an aid to increasing their clairvoyant abilities. It is said to delay ageing and to lengthen life.

*Mother-of-Pearl* (pearly white with pink, green and blue lights): Excellent for protection and brings good luck in romantic and business matters.

*Pearl*: Pearls symbolise the moon, water and the universe and are the stones of mysticism and spirituality. They attract harmony in relationships and good luck financially. Excellent for developing psychic abilities.

*Peridot, chrysolite, olivine* (green or greenish-gold, transparent): Ruled by the planet Venus, so it relates to all matters of the heart. It soothes nervousness and helps dispel negative emotions such as anger, grief, etc. It deflects negativity directed at the owner, so is excellent for protection. It strengthens eyesight and increases clairvoyant abilities. It attracts love and wealth and dispels anger.

*Quartz, crystal* (clear, colourless stone): Also known as rock crystal, these crystals have been held to be sacred by ancient cultures, such as the Egyptians, Greeks and Romans, and also by the Tibetans and native American Indians. Crystals have the power to attract, store, amplify and transmit energy. They are also all-powerful healing stones, helping in all forms of illness, physical and mental. Quartz crystal helps to develop self-confidence and stimulates psychic and clairvoyant abilities. It attracts good luck and good health. This is the stone of psychics and healers and has become very popular as jewellery in recent times, commonly worn as a pendant around the neck. Works extremely well when charged.

*Quartz, rose* (warm pink): The stone of love and romance, friendship and attraction. It is exchanged by lovers to strengthen the bond of love. It attracts love and friendship to the lonely and promotes peace and harmony in relationships. It also has purifying qualities and clears negative vibrations from property when used with clear calcite/snow quartz. Very soothing for sprains and muscular aches and pains.

*Quartz, snow* (white like snow): This powerful stone increases psychic powers and healing energies. It has soothing and calming qualities and helps relieve stress and tension. It increases self-control, so is an excellent aid to slimming, giving up smoking, etc. A powerful stone for clearing spirit presences and for the purification and clearing of energies in houses and buildings. Works well combined with calcite and/or rose quartz.

*Quartz, sun* (golden orange): The stone of wisdom and peace, it helps combat indecisiveness and stimulates cosmic consciousness. It is a powerful healer and helps in depression as well as with digestive problems, diabetes and constipation.

*Rhodonite* (light pink, veined with black): A stone of love, energy and peace, its pink tones warm and soothe the heart. Helps develop balance and harmony of mind, body and spirit. Helps develop clarity of thought in times of confusion. It also attracts love to the wearer and develops psychic powers.

*Sphalerite* (white with black and shiny silver inclusions): A stone of the emotions, the psychic mind, love and healing. Said to lengthen life and preserve health, it also aids recovery from emotional upset. It is a powerful aid for discovering hidden talents and realising potential.

*Sugilite/Suganite* (purple): A dense stone favoured by professional psychics and healers, it is an invaluable aid to meditation and all forms of creative work.

*Topaz* (transparent, ranges from pale yellow to deep golden orange): This is an exceptionally lucky stone, attracting success in business and financial matters. It also attracts love and romance to the wearer and increases harmony and balance in business and romantic relationships. Has strong protective powers for the wearer, especially against fire and accidents. Placed under the pillow at night, it banishes nightmares and ends sleep-walking. Relieves the pain of rheumatism and arthritis and increases self-confidence, positive energy and motivation.

*Tourmaline, black:* This is the stone for problems of the nervous system, being very effective in preventing and controlling faintness and dizziness. It protects from all sorts of negative influences and energises and gives balance. An excellent stone for attracting friendship, it also helps in developing psychic powers.

*Tourmaline, green*: Attracts money and success in business. It also has powerful healing energies, reducing headaches, inflammations and epileptic seizures. It also stimulates creativity.

*Turquoise* (blue or blue/green): Traditionally the stone of protection, this is a powerful healing stone. It strengthens the eyes, reduces fever and soothes headaches. Helps to prevent migraine when worn next to the skin. It is a lucky stone to give to a loved one, promoting harmony and fidelity. Wearing turquoise is said to attract friends, make one happy and increase one's beauty. Good for the eyes, neck, chest, lungs and heart.

**CHAPTER 10**

# Seeing into the Past

IRELAND HAS A WEALTH of ancient monuments, some of which date back to pre-historic times. Among the earliest settlers were a 'megalithic' people, a word which is derived from the Greek *megas*, meaning large, and *lithos*, meaning a stone. Their traces can be found all over the country in cromlechs, logan stones, stone circles, dolmens and chambered tumuli. It seemed to me a logical progression to turn my interest from crystals and gemstones to these stones and to conclude that, if small pieces of stone can absorb energy, large stones and stone structures could do the same.

I began by seeking out and feeling ancient stone monuments to see if I could get any 'vibes' from them. This is called 'psychometrising', that is, absorbing feelings through the palms of the hands in order to receive information about the past of the object held.

Anyone can practise this. First, it is necessary to have an object to work with, usually a piece of jewellery or a watch belonging to another person. Close your eyes and will yourself to relax and begin the primary breathing, holding the object you wish to psychometrise in the centre of the palm of your left hand (the receptive hand, as you want to receive information through the palm *chakra*. Some find it works better to hold the object against the third eye.

Tune into the skin on your palm, picturing it as full of sensors searching for information about the object resting there. Information will come to you in a variety of ways. You may 'see' pictures, images or symbols in your mind's eye. Impressions or thoughts may come into your mind. Less often you may 'hear' words or sentences. It helps to focus your energy if you tell yourself: I want to know about this ring, etc.

Of course, the information you receive will tend to be about the owner or wearer of the object, and so it could appear nonsensical when you are new to this technique. It is not important to interpret what you receive but to pass it on with confidence to the person who owns the object.

For example, when I was first fascinated by the concept of psychometry, a friend brought me a leather wallet and asked if I could 'get any vibes', saying that it belonged to her ex-boyfriend. As I held it, I got an image of an old lady who was blind in one eye, which made no sense to me in the context of what I had been told. I mentioned this to my friend, who seemed puzzled at first, but then remembered that her 'ex' had told her the wallet had belonged originally to his old nanny. He had kept it as a keepsake when she died.

I then saw what appeared to be a beautiful, sweeping back garden with a high stone wall at the end. I could sense, rather than see, that a train track ran beyond and parallel to the wall. This turned out to be an exact description of the garden of the house she had lived in with her 'ex' in London.

Often when working with a personal item such as jewellery you may receive impressions of a personality or of emotions, for example, a feeling of sadness or anger. I have found any form of impression you receive will tend to make some sort of sense to the person you are psychometrising for, so it really is important to have the confidence to say what you see, feel or sense.

The use of psychometry is not confined to small, inanimate objects. You can gain impressions from trees, plants even animals. I discovered accidentally that I could receive impressions from the mind of a cat by touching his head to my third eye. My blue Burmese, Hermes, jumped on my lap one day and pushed his face against mine in a gesture of affection and I got a glimpse of a grey, hazy image. I deliberately rested my forehead against his and focused my energy. I received blurred, black and grey images of gliding through long grass and an earthy smell filled my nostrils. I felt I must be reading my pet's mind.

Sometimes people find it easier to psychometrise through the third eye than through the palms of the hands and I have also found that the spine is capable of receiving powerful impressions from trees and from standing stones. I remember as a child sitting on the sand with my back against a large rock at the edge of Johnstown beach in Co. Wexford, seeing roughly-dressed men carrying a wooden boat towards the sea. I was about eight years old at the time and widely known to have a 'vivid imagination', so no-one paid any attention to my tale of 'wild men with a boat'.

When I began researching the type of information that could be elicited through psychometry, the first observation I made was that, while all stones contained energy, they did not all transmit it, some of them acting as receivers. In every stone circle I have visited, I found that the stones alternate, every second stone being a transmitter or 'male' stone, the others being receptive or 'female' stones. The ancient peoples who positioned these stones were obviously in tune with the natural energies inherent in them and, in a sense, with harnessing these energies. Female energy is receptive, passive and lunar (the energy of the moon) while male energy is projective, active and solar, being the energy of the sun.

When it came to psychometrising specific stones, however, I must confess to some disappointment, in the sense that I did not experience the intensity of vibrations from them that I had anticipated. One of my first experiments was at Newgrange in Co. Meath which, according to folklore, was the fairy palace of Aonghus, a prince of the Tuatha Dé Danaan, and part of the Boyne complex of neolithic passage graves. I spent some time at this ancient site in an attempt to gain some knowledge of the builders.

Being inside the inner chamber of the mound feels like being inside a womb and I sensed instinctively that this place had been used for rites connected with fertility and birth, as well as with death and burial. I then tuned into the energies of the place and the first image I received was of a band of warriors breaking into the chamber in search of a hide-out. Subsequently, in reading about Newgrange, I discovered a reference to the plundering of the monument by Danes in the ninth century and I am sure that this is what I was seeing that day.

As I meditated longer, I had an experience which was far more satisfying than the earlier one. I saw a young girl, probably in her early teens, dressed in a grey-blue calf-length tunic, tied at the waist with what appeared to be gold wires. She was

## Seeing into the Past

sitting with a bunch of mistletoe beside her and was stripping the berries from the twigs and putting them into two neat piles. She carefully put the berries into a little basket, laid three twigs on the ground and then scattered the rest of the twigs over them in a seemingly random way, a slight frown wrinkling her brow. That is all I saw, but I believe she was a druidess practising an ancient form of divination, using the druids' sacred plant, the mistletoe.

Another of my psychometrising experiments was on the Hill of Tara, also in Co. Meath. This was the seat of the High Kings of Ireland and the ancient power centre of the druids. On one of the mounds at Tara is a *dallán* or standing stone, twelve feet long but with only about half that above the ground. This is reputed to be the *Lia Fáil*, on which the High Kings were inaugurated and it is the subject of many legends. Psychometrising this stone yielded a disappointingly meagre selection of non-specific images. It seems that only a random minority of stones yield significant information. A possible explanation is that famous sites such as Newgrange and Tara attract many visitors and the energy-impression they leave behind somehow dilutes the ancient energies of the place or object.

However, I had more feed-back during a recent experiment in the valley of Kilcoole in Co. Wicklow. Here there is a dolmen-shaped stone edifice known as the 'druids' altar'. One sunny afternoon in May 1993, I visited the site and spent some time psychometrising the stones of the dolmen and some of the nearby trees. I realised at once that this was not a genuine burial house, as many dolmens are, but a structure resembling one and used for ceremonial purposes.

I used first my hands and then my spine to tune in to the energies of the stones. The first visual impressions I received were the normal 'first layer' images, as I call them, which I get when psychometrising most objects, large or small. These appear as random images, usually of people or animals who have been in the place. I look for clues, such as the type of clothes worn, to tell me whether it is an ancient or modern image I am receiving. First layer images tend to be modern impressions, the longer I concentrate, the further back I appear to go in time. It feels like peeling off layers of time. In this case, as my breathing took me deeper into trance, I consciously opened my mind to receive information from those who had formerly occupied the site. I sat down beside the stones with my back against a large oak, a tree revered by the ancient druids as a symbol of long life and strength, and 'heard' them plan a sacrifice. The victim was a young man who had been caught stealing and I am not sure whether he was being punished or used for ceremonial purposes but he seemed to be resigned to his fate.

The stones of the 'altar' themselves yielded images of what appeared to be a fertility ceremony of some sort, involving small animals, like rabbits or hares. A nearby tree 'showed' me a woman tying one end of a rope, made of twisted reeds and twigs, around 'my' tree and the other end to another tree. She was dressed in a long tunic almost to her ankles, with vertical stripes of different colours, and was singing or chanting softly as she worked. I felt there was some ceremonial significance to this action, as it was done in an almost reverent way. I felt she was 'marrying' pairs of trees.

Then I noticed that she was being watched by another woman who stood nearby, with one arm round the trunk of the tree in whose shadow she stood. Looking around, I saw eleven other women forming a circle, each standing beside an oak tree with her right arm around its trunk. They watched silently as the first woman moved silently among the trees, selecting apparently random pairs of trees and joining them with her leafy ropes. The images faded before I could examine each women in detail but I felt I was watching a ceremony performed by druidesses, a form of communion with the trees. It is possible that the trees represented couples, as I felt there was a fertility connection in the ritual I observed.

Traces of the druids can be found in many parts of Ireland, one being Killiney Hill, near where I live. Here there is another 'druids' altar' and this report of a psychic experience was given me by Terry Ralph, one of Ireland's leading hairdressers. When he was about thirteen years old, he went with his older brother and some friends to the altar, which is hidden behind an old L-shaped stone wall.

As he came near, Terry experienced an overpowering energy which seemed to come from behind the wall, from the altar itself. He stared at the wall and felt he could see through it to the sea beyond. He confesses to being scared out of his wits when he saw a group of twelve or fourteen young men with shaven heads and wearing long white robes. They were arranged in a zig-zag formation and were dancing in a circle from left to right. The whole experience lasted some ten minutes. His companions could see nothing and began to tease him but decided to leave the place which was causing him so much distress.

Another friend, an actor called Keith Patrick Gaskin, had a similar experience at the Piper's Stones, a stone circle near Baltinglass in Co. Wicklow. He had climbed up the hill and sat down to catch his breath, leaning his back against one of the stones. Suddenly the air became, in his words, 'charged with electricity' and his sight seemed to grow hazy. Then he saw six young men, dressed in robes of different colours, walking away from him down the hill with brisk, purposeful strides. They were gone in a moment. Keith felt quite shaken afterwards and was in no doubt that this was a genuine clairvoyant vision. I judge it to be a case of 'spontaneous psychometry', which is experienced by a great many people who have no idea what is happening to them.

I regularly receive reports similar to Keith's and Terry's from people who have no special interest in psychic matters. I tell them they can try to channel this ability consciously in order to receive information about specific places and things, both through psychometry and meditation. I use both these methods myself and almost always get some form of impression coming through. Sometimes I do this before or after visiting a place. This is a type of 'remote viewing', a psychic skill with which the practitioner 'sends' his or her mind to another place to receive visual and mental impressions.

Ireland is full of sites which hold the energies of ancient times. Every one of us has at some time come across a place or a river or hill which evoked a strong emotional feeling, convincing us that it was somehow 'different'. Often, without knowing it, we are at a confluence of two or more ley lines, which are ancient pathways generally connecting the main physical features of the ancient landscape, created in a time when man spontaneously psychometrised his surroundings. These ancient power-lines can be recognised by anyone attuned to such things. Psychometry gives us the ability to go one step further and possibly identify or define exactly what it is about the place that is causing the effect experienced. Just open your mind to the flow of the earth's energies and you may tune in to amazing sights, sounds and even smells of the past.

## CHAPTER 11

# 'Tuning in' to County Wicklow

IN MY TRAVELS AROUND IRELAND, I have found the greatest concentration of earth energies and psychic phenomena to be found in Co. Wicklow, where most of my leisure time is spent and where I hope to live some day. Since childhood, I have had numerous experiences in different parts of the county. In Glendalough, a sacred place of the druids before it became a famous monastic settlement, I heard the monks chant one evening as I sat contemplating the beauty of the lakes.

Bray, the largest town in the county, is a busy seaside resort with a cosmopolitan flavour in the summer. Visiting tourists might find it hard to believe that only a stone's throw away from the beach where children play and eat candy-floss, I cleared a peeping-tom poltergeist from a house. This particular spirit was making the three female inhabitants of the house nervous by watching them in the bathroom. Each of them had sensed someone watching them while they washed or showered but thought it was imagination and never mentioned it to either of the others. Only when the thirteen-year-old daughter of the house was overheard telling her friend about it did it emerge that everyone except the husband of the house had noticed it. We decided that Tom (as we christened the spirit, of course) had no interest in men. However, it is possible that the husband in question might not have noticed even if he was being watched, as some people are less sensitive than others to spirit energy.

In Arklow, a town famous for its pottery, I performed my one and only boat clearing. A very embarrassed fisherman contacted me as a result of hearing me on the radio and asked me what I could do to help him. A mischievous spirit had the annoying habit of throwing the seaman's possessions overboard. He would put something down only to see it fly into the water.

I made incomplete contact with this particular spirit, who seemed to be an old man, but the healing I performed on him appears to have worked as there have been no further incidents since my visit.

Another 'watery' spirit I dealt with was in the goldfish pond of a rambling old garden at the back of a nineteenth-century cottage in Blessington. The atmosphere around the pool was far from pleasant. Although situated in a sunny spot, the water always looked as though it were in deep shadow and anyone who sat near it felt an awful depression descend on them. I worked on the place for only a few minutes before realising it was cleared, which took me by surprise, as it is definitely one of the most intensely sad places I have ever visited.

It would seem logical to suppose that the stronger the negative energy feels in a place, the more positive energy it will require to clear it. Strangely enough this does not appear to be the case. This puzzled me for many years, until I realised that the human factor is what is significant. In the same way that some people are more receptive than others to psychic healing, some spirits are also more receptive.

In this case, the spirit was that of a very old woman who was waiting for her son to return from the war. She had been told he was dead but was convinced that someone had made a mistake. I managed to persuade her that I could send her off to meet him instead. Her spirit felt weary and dreadfully depressed but she was gone almost the instant I began sending out healing. I felt completely drained after working on her though I had been bubbling with energy ten minutes before.

I have visited the house several times since and that little pond is now a happy, sunny spot. The owner of the house believes her goldfish have benefited as well, as they have virtually doubled in size since I worked on the pond.

In Kilpeddar in Co. Wicklow, I encountered a spirit I call the 'Welcome Spirit'. He resides in MacDyers pub, also known as the Kilpeddar Inn. This case was the subject of a BBC Ulster programme when the pub was visited by myself and Seán Rafferty, the BBC presenter. We were told tales of the pub coming alive at night with sounds of tinkling glasses and banging doors when the family were in bed at night. An old, bent, white-haired man was seen by a member of the family, standing in the small snug which is the oldest part of the building. I saw him myself immediately I entered the room, and felt I could easily contact and send him on. To my surprise, however, when it came to removing him from the premises, the family agreed at the last minute that they wanted him to stay!

The part of Co. Wicklow which has provided me with the richest supply of psychic experiences is the area round

Kilcoole, where I witnessed the vision, which I have already described, of the druidesses' ceremony round the oak trees. Present-day Kilcoole is probably best-known in Ireland as the location of 'Glenroe', a fictitious town in which the TV soap of the same name is set. It is a quiet, friendly village, pretty and peaceful, and I must admit it left me unprepared for the tales of brutality I was to uncover about its past.

Near the village, there is a place called the Fortress Rock which myself and a companion explored one day. I sat down and had begun to meditate, when a roaring, thunderous sound filled my ears and I discerned a series of images of warriors doing battle round me. I could distinguish two different groups. One consisted of tall, big-boned men, mostly fair-haired and with fair complexions. The other group was of smaller, darker-skinned and more muscular-looking men with brown hair of different shades.

The colours they wore were different, too, though I did not have much time to notice as the images lasted no more than a few seconds. At one stage, I smelt the smoke of smouldering timber and I got the impression of a small wooden building, attached to a larger structure, beginning to burn. The taller warriors appeared to be the attackers while the smaller fighters were trying to drive them away from the hill and the surrounding area.

My companion, who has lived in the area all his life, was extremely interested in what I reported and promised to do some research on the area to see if he could shed any light on what I had seen. As we were leaving the Rock, I mentioned casually that I noticed a missing hill, pointing to the direction where I had distinctly seen a hill when watching the ancient battle. My companion reacted with shock and amazement;

there had indeed been a hill where I was pointing. It had since been worn away by erosion. Very few people were aware of this fact, my friend said, and he seemed shaken and, for the first time, totally convinced of my psychic abilities.

After that, my friend took me to many places that had strange reputations in the area. I visited an old house where I pointed to a wall and said, 'That seems to be hollow.' It was indeed, for this strong-looking wall concealed a tunnel through which the occupants of the house could escape in times of trouble. In the cellars of the same house, I saw an old wooden boat which I described to my companion. From my description, he thought I might have seen a Viking boat.

Recently I had a 'phone call from my friend to tell me some exciting news. In the course of work on the house and land in question, foundations of an old dwelling place had been found. It appears to have been the home of a Viking chieftain, so my friend's intuitive guess about the boat appears to have been correct. In another part of the huge cellar, I told my companion that babies had been murdered and buried under the ground there by their own parents. One of the men working on the estate verified that this had, indeed, happened in the house in the Middle Ages. In another part of Kilcoole, I have seen slaves being brought upriver from the sea by men in the robes of olden times.

One day, my friend from Kilcoole brought me a bundle of papers, photocopies of old maps and manuscripts connected with the area, in the hope of shedding some light on the battle I had seen at the Fortress Rock. The one which interested me was entitled 'The Destruction of Da Derga's Hostel'. One of the few complete long narratives still in existence in ancient Irish literature, it told the story of Conaire Mór, High King of

Ireland, who was slain in a fierce battle in what I believe is the very spot where I had my vision. The hostel in the story existed probably about the year A.D. 50.

One of the interesting facts I learned about Kilcoole is that two of its ancient churches – Kilfornock and Kilpatrick – are no longer to be found. On the banks of the Leabeg river, I saw glimpses of a church which I believe to be the lost church of Kilfornock. I also saw activity which led me to believe that this had been an ancient trade route, and this was later confirmed by my historian friend. The present church at Kilquade was built in the late 1400s by a gallowglass (Scottish mercenary) called MacQuade. It was subsequently destroyed by Cromwell and rebuilt by the Fitzgeralds, a prominent family of the area. It was destroyed again in 1798 but the Catholic church got compensation for it from the British government and it was rebuilt in 1801. I believe that this is the site of the missing Kilpatrick Church.

While I had seen an ancient battle take place at the rock of Kilcoole, the area has also seen fighting in more recent years. The year 1798 is well-known in Irish history as the year the rebellion of the United Irishmen took place. As a result of my research in the area, I found that many of the historic figures of the region are still causing problems for the present-day inhabitants of parts of Co. Wicklow. Many of the houses I have been called out to 'clear' have turned out to be formerly inhabited by notorious characters from the pages of history. Troubled humans make troubled spirits, I fear.

Almost all the land in Ireland in the 1700s was owned by Protestants of British origin. Fearing a revolution in Ireland, they began to organise local defence forces, known as the militia and the yeomanry. Both forces were noted for the brutality they used in their attempts to suppress the growth of the United Irishmen. Although the officers of these forces were Protestant many Catholics joined the ranks. The government did not trust these men to serve in their own areas, so transferred them as far from home as possible to prevent favouritism. The leader of the Yeomanry in the Kilcoole/Newtownmountkennedy region was the infamous Captain Archer. The inhuman atrocities perpetrated on the people of Wicklow by Archer and his men were unbelievable.

On 11 May 1798, Lieutenant-Colonel Peter Craig issued a proclamation forbidding the possession of any form of weapon and the people were ordered to hand up anything that could be used as a weapon, including scythes, reaping hooks and shillelaghs. The yeomanry were zealous in the extreme in their hunting-out and seizing of 'weapons' from the people. A common punishment inflicted on transgressors was to be flogged until nearly dead, then half-hanged and 'picketed' for three days. Picketing was the practice of making the victim stand on one naked foot on a pointed stake. Torture of every description was carried out by Archer and his men, but the Captain himself met a cruel and untimely end. He was kicked to death by his favourite horse, his skull smashed to pieces and his brain scattered on the road. A violent death for a violent man, but I believe his spirit still roams the Wicklow area to the south of Newtownmountkennedy where he had his home. Many reports of strange phenomena lead me to this conclusion.

The former home of Griffin Jones, one of Archer's thugs, was demolished many years ago and a large, local authority housing estate now stands in its place. Over the last few years, there have been reports of spirit activity – footsteps, banging doors, 'cold spots', etc., from several of the houses. While I was reading about the area I stumbled across the information that Jones had been a former tenant and I believe it is his spirit that has been causing disturbances in the area.

Orna lives with her nine-year-old son in this housing estate near Newtownmountkennedy. She contacted me to say she was sure there was a 'wandering soul' in her house and she asked if I could do anything about it. We agreed a date and time and I went to visit her accompanied by my friend, Ronan McKenna We arrived at the house to find Orna very upset. Her car keys were missing and she was late to collect her son from school. 'I always put them on the hall table and they are always being moved when Conor's in school and I'm on my own in the house – there's no-one here to move them.' Ronan found the keys hidden behind a cushion (the pupil being better than the teacher?) and when Orna had collected Conor and dropped him to her mother's, she sat down to tell us her story.

Orna had been living in the house for a year, and right from the start had taken a dislike to the larger of the front bedrooms. 'It always feels cold and unfriendly, as though something is in there, watching you.'

She had frequently heard muffled thumps coming from the room at night, but thought it might be because the radiator was switched off. She thought it strange that she heard the noises in summer when the central heating was switched off. Once, when in the hall, she heard a loud creak upstairs and, as she turned, a coat 'flew at me' from its peg on the wall. 'It didn't drop down, it flew across the hall at me.' On three occasions one Christmas, she heard footsteps in the attic above her room.

I had the distinct impression that an unpleasant male presence was inhabiting the house, although I could not see him clearly. I worked in the house for about two hours, and in the six months since the clearing, no further incidents have been reported. Another housing estate in the same area has four houses where the inhabitants all report spirit activity and another recently built estate is already yielding similar stories.

Archer's right-hand man, Corporal George Kennedy, was a Catholic whose name to this day provokes fear and loathing around Kilcoole. In life, he was an outcast hated by his own people. In death, he was interred in the old churchyard of Kilcoole where nothing grows over his heart on his grave. I must confess I was sceptical when I heard this but I have been to the grave in summer, when the entire graveyard has been overgrown with weeds. I have read the headstone of Corporal George Kennedy and seen with my own eyes the large bare patch of earth that is almost half the length of the grave. Sceptics down through the years have planted a variety of seeds and plants and many have sought a logical explanation but still the patch of earth over Kennedy's heart remains bare.

Captain Archer's other trusted aide was Samuel Lesley (or Livesley) also known as 'Bob' or 'Smug'. His gravestone in Newcastle churchyard gives his address as the house I refer to as Kilcoole's 'House of Many Spirits'.

**CHAPTER 12**

# The House of Many Spirits

I HAD A 'PHONE CALL ONE DAY early in April 1993 from a gentleman called Seán. I listened with growing interest as he told me of a wide range of phenomena occurring in his home, Ballyshane Farm in Co. Wicklow.

Ten years earlier, a short BBC television documentary had revealed that a large number of witnesses had experienced strange things both in the house and on the surrounding land. Moving objects, strange footsteps and unexplained noises were all described to me as well as apparitions of a most intriguing nature. I made arrangements to visit the house and its owners as soon as possible.

First I contacted Bernard Evans, who had been with me in the case described in Chapter 6. He was very keen to accompany me so we decided to go the following Monday. From the moment I made the arrangement, the problems started. The night before the proposed visit, I suddenly developed a raging temperature and sore throat and reluctantly 'phoned to cancel the appointment.

*The House of Many Spirits*

Next day at lunchtime I received a call from Seán: 'They're going mad out here,' he said and told me that the house had been alive with phenomena all morning. One of his children had been hurled violently against the kitchen table. Doors were banging all over the house and footsteps were heard in empty rooms. The children were under the table playing with an unseen 'friend' and their nanny, Marian, caught a glimpse of a grey shadow, the first time she had had any visible evidence that the children were not imagining things.

I reassured Seán as best I could, promising to send some 'absent healing' to the house and its inhabitants and promising to be there in three days' time, no matter what happened. I still felt pretty ill on the Thursday but decided I was going and made arrangements to pick Bernard Evans up at midday. As soon as I started the car, I realised something was up: I had a flat tyre. I made it as far as my local tyre centre at Shankill, where I explained the urgency of my situation. The mechanic dropped everything, promising to have me on the road in a few minutes. Then he looked at the tyres and said: 'This house you're going to – something doesn't want you to get there.' He pointed to my tyres, two of which were punctured.

However, I was soon on the way, almost half-an-hour later than planned. I collected Bernard and soon we were heading for Kilcoole. Following Seán's directions, we found the house easily enough. It was a large, sprawling building at the end of a long drive, set in wide, rolling grounds, surrounded by farmland. Seán greeted us at the door, a handsome man with sparkling blue eyes and an engaging personality. He introduced his children and their nanny, who looked after them while their mother, Liz, was at work.

Over lunch, Seán told us a little of the history of the house where he had grown up. It had originally been built in the 1700s, rebuilding and additions were carried out in 1870 and again in 1930. Between 1890 and 1920, the house was owned by Colonel (later Sir Frederick) Wrench whose land stewart, James McKee, lived there with his family. In 1947, a Dutchman called Van Reek, who was suspected of being a Nazi collaborator during the Second World War, moved in and lived there until Seán's family took possession.

Seán showed Bernard and myself round the house and said he had experienced unusual occurrences in it for as long as he could remember. He also gave me diaries in which he had recorded a daily account of incidents. Other members of the family told me about their experiences. As is usual in cases of this kind, I found that they spoke with some hesitancy, as though they did not expect to be taken seriously. I find that most people are embarrassed by psychic phenomena and feel there must be something 'wrong' with them. This is why I find it necessary sometimes to give healing to people living in a house where there is spirit activity.

Seán described an incident long before he was married, when he was about twenty. He was woken early one morning at about 4 a.m. by a jingling sound coming from a bedside locker. Leaning over to check what was making the noise, he saw the fold-up alarm clock turning round and moving back and forth by itself. It then moved to the floor as though lifted down by unseen hands and continued to move around as if a child were playing with it.

According to Seán, when the house was 'acting up', several people would report odd happenings though not everyone heard or saw the same thing. At one stage, however, there was a spate of electrical problems which lasted for several weeks.

## The House of Many Spirits

Four light-bulbs blew at the same time in three different rooms. On occasions, the TV would go dead, only to switch itself on again several hours later. A tape-recorder sometimes picked up a radio programme and the vacuum cleaner and central heating seemed to have minds of their own, working only when they felt like it. Seán called in an electrician who checked everything thoroughly and was satisfied there was no logical explanation for what was occurring.

The children's rooms were the centre of many other happenings reported by various members and friends of the family. The nanny, Marian, told me that when she started work in the house in 1989 something stopped her entering one of the bedrooms. 'At first, it was just a feeling I got when I went to go in the door of the children's bedroom. Then I started seeing "him", an old, grumpy-looking man. He would lift up his walking-stick and wave it at me to stop me from going into the room.' Every night for two weeks, the girl had a nightmare about the man. He looked as if he was in his seventies, had dark, menacing brown eyes and was wearing black trousers, a black waistcoat without a jacket and a military-looking hat. The portrayal tallied exactly with the description Seán's mother gave me of the house's former inhabitant, Van Reek.

Twice in one night in February 1993, Seán's three-year-old son woke up terrified with nightmares, acting as though scared of someone in the room. On numerous other occasions, when the children were fast asleep, sounds of children playing were heard from their rooms. Often loud thumps occurred, causing the parents to believe one of the children had fallen out of bed when, in fact, they were asleep. Windows and doors were heard to open and shut and door-knobs to turn, though everything was all right when checked. Marian would frequently hear childish footsteps running from the children's room to the bathroom or to the parent's bedroom. Sometimes, when she turned on the radio to drown out the noises, it would switch itself off and refuse to play.

One night, friends of the family slept in the boys' room. At about 1.30 a.m. the wife sensed a hand resting on her hip and was transfixed with fear as she felt herself being pulled, feet first, towards the window. She jumped up and the sensation stopped, so she tried to go back to sleep. All was quiet for a time and then she heard a rustling noise in the corner of the room, like the sound of clothes moving about. She woke her husband, who told her she was imagining things and, when no further disturbances occurred, she finally went back to sleep.

Marian also said she felt a 'bad' presence several times in the kitchen. On one occasion, she was in the kitchen with the children when a drawer in the dresser opened and a rolling-pin jumped out, followed seconds later by the rest of the contents. On another occasion, the three-year-old child of the family went to climb onto an empty chair in the kitchen and suddenly flew backwards as if pushed by unseen hands. 'The lady pushed me,' he bawled, looking fearfully in the direction of the chair. He described her as wearing a long, pink dress and having brown hair. She seemed to be the only female spirit inhabiting Ballyshane Farm, as all the others I encountered were male.

On one particularly wet day, Seán's son kept telling Marian that 'the boy is looking in the window and wants to come in out of the rain to play.' Marian looked out to where the child was pointing but could see nothing. A few minutes later, she heard a whimpering sound coming from outside. She opened the door but nothing was there. Whenever he was questioned, Seán's son said the invisible boy was his friend who came to play with him. The child was reluctant to say much but he described the boy as having brown hair and wearing a black jacket and trousers and red shoes.

Marian came to know instinctively when 'the boy' was around. There would be a cold breeze in the room, drawers and cupboard doors would open suddenly, pictures on the wall would move as if touched by invisible hands. On one occasion, a mug 'flew' from the shelf above the kitchen sink while a can of fly-spray on the counter beneath shook furiously for several minutes. Each time the children would say 'the boy' was responsible.

Marian's friend, Anna, also had many experiences in the house. She, too, sometimes heard footsteps, banging doors and loud noises from the children's rooms though no-one was there. One day, she was in the kitchen with Anna and the children while Seán was on the telephone talking to me. I was telling him about an English poltergeist who had been asked for money by one of the people he was annoying. 'The next thing a five-pound note came floating through the air straight into the guy's hand,' I told Seán. 'You should try that; ask yours to bring you some money. Make them do some good for a change.' Meanwhile, Anna was saying goodbye to Marian at the kitchen door when the pocket of her jeans turned inside out, and her money appeared at Seán's feet. Next time Anna visited the house, her handbag opened of its own accord and she had to grab her money to prevent it spilling out.

On numerous occasions, partial manifestations, mostly of children, were seen. When a new swing was put up in the back garden, several shadowy little figures were seen clustering around it and one was even seen swinging on it. One day, Anna sat in the kitchen, with her daughter on her knee, talking to Marian. Seán's son looked out the window and said: 'There's a man at the door,' but there was no-one to be seen. Suddenly, out of the corner of her eye, Anna noticed the grey, shadowy figure of a child begin to materialise and move around on the floor. This is one of the few occasions when Anna was badly shaken by her experiences in the house. She was normally quite matter-of-fact about her experiences.

Marian's boyfriend, Jason, was originally very sceptical about all the stories he had heard. One night, however, as he drove home on his new motor-cycle after dropping Marian off at the farmhouse, he saw a young boy running across the road. He swerved to avoid him but knocked him down. Sick with worry, he jumped off the bike and went back to look for the boy. The road was empty so he began to search the ditches and roadside vegetation. A passing motorist stopped to help him but they could find no trace of the boy.

Jason decided to go on home. As he drove over a hump-back bridge spanning the river on Ballyshane Farm land, he saw a child with dark, curly hair and dressed in what looked like a long 'old-fashioned night-shirt' standing in the middle of the road. He was staring malevolently at Jason, as if daring him to run into him. Jason swerved as before but this time the child disappeared before his astonished eyes. Since then, Jason had avoided driving in the area after dark.

The most outstanding incident in the history of spirit activity in the house concerns a large mid-summer barbecue given by the family in the late 1970s. The party went on late and most of the guests decided to spend the night at the farm. At about 7 a.m. the sleepers had a rude awakening as the sound of children playing filled the air, despite the fact that the younger members of the family had been sent to stay with friends for the night. All over the house, windows were opened and comments shouted down to the plum tree in the garden below where the children could be heard playing. One of the visitors looked down and saw nothing. Another saw shadowy shapes of children who seemed to be flying in and out of the branches of the tree. 'I could hear them clearly but could barely make out their outlines,' she said.

Three members of the family as well as numerous guests had seen more. Looking down from the bedroom windows onto the wide lawn with its tall purple-flowering plum tree, a merry-go-round was seen, full of ghostly children. It was described as being like a wooden wheel on top of a post, with four ropes hanging from it on which children were swinging. It appeared in some way to be part of the tree itself. One witness said she couldn't understand how the children seemed to 'glide through' the branches of the tree without hurting themselves. Other witnesses saw children running round the tree, shouting up to those on the merry-go-round.

The episode attracted a lot of interest at the time but was soon forgotten. Several years later, Seán decided to cut down the plum tree which by now was blocking the light into the living-room. He showed me what had come to light when they chopped down the tree – it is still there to be seen. Tangled in the roots was the base of an old merry-go-round!

Seán went on to tell me that the unusual occurrences in the house had really escalated around the time the river running through the property was being widened. Bernard and I decided to go to the river and record a conversation with Seán there for radio. Just before we set out, Bernard discovered that his tape-recorder had been switched on accidentally and the batteries were dead. Fortunately he had spares and we walked to the river bank.

As we prepared for the recording, Bernard then discovered that the small battery powering his microphone and the cap holding it in had dropped out on the way. We couldn't find them anywhere and had to go back to the house for a replacement battery and a piece of sellotape to seal it in. Retracing our steps to the river, we found the missing battery and cap on the ground. It was interesting to note that nobody made any comment, except for Bernard's non-committal remark that it was 'weird the way the batteries were all acting up today'.

Seán is a born storyteller and we listened spellbound to his recital of events connected with the farm. Shortly after work had begun on the river, Seán's mother woke one night to see a child standing at the foot of the bed. Thinking it to be one of her many grandchildren, she told him to go back to his own room. Next morning, she recalled that the child's night-shirt and hair had appeared to be soaking wet. On checking, she realised it had not been any of her family and dismissed the whole matter as a dream. Since then, however, the same child has been seen both by her and by other members of the family, always with wet hair. I believe this is the spirit of a child who was drowned in the river at some stage, possibly that of young Thomas McKee, whose family had lived in Ballyshane Farm before Seán moved in. Later that day, we saw his grave in Newcastle churchyard. The headstone records his death in 1902 at the age of ten years.

Seán then brought us into a modern office annexe and asked me did I get any impressions from the room. 'Someone died here,' I told him, gesturing with my hand towards a spot on the ground. He then told me that a young man had shot himself in that room a few years before and that I was pointing to the exact spot where his body had been found.

## The House of Many Spirits

The next place we visited was a large wooden tree-house where many children had seen a young boy who appeared to different children to be just about their own age, whether they were three or four or any age up to about ten years. I also believe he was the boy Seán's children enjoyed playing with under the table.

Later, at nearby Newcastle cemetery, we saw the graves of former inhabitants of the farm. As we were reading the McKee family headstone, which listed the name of young Thomas McKee, we were surprised by a shout from Seán's sister, Sarah, who had accompanied us. She pointed to one of the headstones – that recording the burial of the infamous Samuel Lesley of Captain Archer's Yeomanry. The address on the stone was Ballyshane Farm.

Seán turned to me with a look of horror on his face. There was silence as we realised the importance of what Sarah had found. I felt intuitively that the spirit of Samuel Lesley was responsible for some of the trouble at the farm and I could tell Seán and Bernard felt the same. 'Smug Lesley in my house!' said Seán, shaking his head in disgust. 'Get rid of him, Sandra, get rid of him.'

As we drove home from Newcastle, I was struck by the enormity of the task facing me. There was more land involved in this 'clearing' than I had ever encountered before, more rooms in the house, more spirits and more human inhabitants to heal. I felt it would take several days' work to 'clear' the house. I had never before worked in any place for more than one day and I was not sure how the spirits would react if I left the house in a partially-cleared state.

For the safety of the family, I decided to work on the more aggressive spirits first and to re-balance the energies of the house on the next day I visited it, leaving the land until later. The appointed day arrived and I made careful preparations for the 'clearing'. I took longer than usual over my positive energy exercises and cleansed and charged a large bag of quartz pieces.

When I arrived at the house, it was peaceful and quiet, although it had been 'going mad', as Seán told me, earlier in the week. I decided to work first on the kitchen which seemed to be dominated by a more negative energy. Having made my preparations, I took a deep breath and tried to contact the spirit of Samuel Lesley. As usual, I was of two minds. On the one hand, I was confident of my ability to heal and help, yet, at the same time, I was reluctant to meet characters like Lesley and Van Reek, even in spirit form.

As I began to send healing, focusing on Samuel Lesley, the room became icy cold and I felt as if a cold wind were coursing through my veins. I began visualising bright, golden sunlight, projecting warm solar energy in waves to the spirit I realised was now present. I saw nothing, just felt waves of negative, cold energy pulsing round my solar plexus. As I concentrated, I felt the cold receding. I sent one last burst of energy and literally saw the energy of the room lighten.

I sensed rather than heard a low grunt, like that of an animal, and sent another blast of healing. I fell back, drained, into the chair and realised my body was soaked with sweat. Out of the corner of my eye, I noticed a faint, dark-grey shadow. It was an elderly man and I felt sure I was gazing at the spirit of Samuel Lesley. He was floating backwards towards the front door, moving rapidly about two feet above the floor. For an instant, dark malevolent eyes met mine and then he was gone.

I was trembling all over and made myself a cup of black coffee to re-charge. After a ten-minute rest, I felt ready to resume. I began to send out healing again, this time concentrating on Van Reek. A loud, hacking cough sounded in my left ear and I knew I had contacted him. I told him I would help him to move on and sent out waves of healing light to assist him on his way. I saw nothing but the coughing gradually diminished and finally stopped and I felt he had moved on peacefully. I looked at my watch. Two hours had passed and yet I felt I had entered the room only minutes before. The kitchen now felt spirit-free but I decided to call in Seán and the others to see what they felt. Immediately on entering the room, Seán turned to me and said: 'They're gone, aren't they? The atmosphere in here is different now.'

I felt at this stage that I should work on the remaining spirits in the children's rooms, the site of many of the disturbances, and after another cup of coffee I headed upstairs to continue my task. The energy in the bedrooms was electric. I could almost hear it crackle as I sat on one of the beds. I 'called' the spirit of the little boy in the way I would try to entice any living child, but for a long time there was no response.

I was beginning to wonder whether my energy was too low at this point to make contact when I felt the atmosphere begin to change. A strange, heavy sadness filled the air and I received faint impressions of a woman and a small boy. They seemed grief-stricken and I felt close to tears, affected by their sorrow. 'I understand. I'm a mother, too,' I heard myself whisper. I felt I was tuning into the grief felt by a mother on losing her favourite son and the sorrow of a son being forced to leave his mother. I felt sure some dreadful tragedy had occurred, probably connected with the river. As I sent out healing, I could sense their sadness receding, like the ebbing tide. It was easy to send thoughts of love to the unfortunate woman and her beautiful son and I believe I felt an answering wave of love reach me as they moved on.

I was aching with exhaustion at this stage so I joined the others in the kitchen where I soon revived, thanks to Liz's wonderful cooking.

I returned the following morning and the house felt at peace. But I was not prepared to take any chances and worked thoroughly around the house and land, re-balancing the energies. Everyone agreed that the previous night had been the most peaceful the house had known for years and all the family had slept undisturbed. Recently, I telephoned Seán. He told me that since my visit there has not been another occurrence of the kind that dominated their lives for so long.

Feed-back of this sort makes all my work worthwhile. Although most of my work involves the living rather than those who have passed on, I feel I have established a good relationship with those in the Otherworld. In my radio work, I tune in to, and predict for, people I have never seen, and tuning in to spirit energies is very similar. To some extent, I consider myself a pioneer of the psychic field in Ireland, and I have daily reminders of how far we have come from the ignorance prevailing over the last few decades. I broadcast with independent radio stations on a weekly basis, mostly as a Psychic Agony Aunt, and in all of my broadcasts the underlying message is clear – use your inner resources, develop your intuition and psychic abilities, heal yourself and those around you.

Ireland is a predominantly Roman Catholic country, and many of my clients from other countries ask if I have any 'problems' with the Church. I can truthfully say that I have never encountered open opposition from any Church. The reason for this, I believe, is that I am very open and public about my work so people can judge for themselves. Because my work advocates paying attention to mind, body and spirit, I actively encourage everyone to incorporate the spiritual dimension into their lives. This is the side of ourselves that we tune in to through meditation, yoga and the exercises described in this book. It is a powerful pool of harmony, balance and contentment which we can tap into to improve the quality of our lives.